The No-Study Solution!

A How-to-Book for Getting Higher Grades on Essays without Studying

By Mark Hopkins

© 2012 by Mark Hopkins
All rights reserved, including the right to reproduce this book or portions thereof in any form whatsoever. For information contact:

Mark Hopkins
PO Box 8323
Huntington Beach, CA 92615

NOTE: If you are a professional teacher or home school your children and seek to license this material for your classroom, please go to www.nostudysolution.com and click on "teacher's corner" for details on how to do that.

Thanks to Surfer Sam's World Famous Surf School, in Huntington Beach, CA for providing the photo on page 77. Contact Sam at http://surfwithsam.com/

Manufactured in the United States of America

TABLE OF CONTENTS

QUICK START — 1

-1. THE GAP — 7

The Gap Between the Teacher and the Test — 7

Being Smart Enough — 9
It is Just a Card Game — 14
The Winning Attitude — 17

0. THE SYSTEM — 21

Game Plan — 21

The Elements — 23
The System Revealed — 24
Real Life Situation — 25
Be Teacher-Focused — 28
Eliminating Stress — 29

1. THINK — 31

1-A How to Think up the Ideas — 32
The Mind Scores more Points than the Pen — 32
The Second Draft is Always Better — 33
The Power of Thinking on Paper — 34
The T-View Outline© — 36
Personalize with Sight, Sound and Touch — 41
Benefits of Using the T-View Outline© — 43

1-B. How to De-BUGS© the Ideas — 44
Unseen Gaps — 44
Breakdowns in Logic — 45
Universal Principles in Play — 49
Finding the Boundaries — 52
Glaring Weaknesses — 54
Potential System Changes — 57

1-C. Defuse the Counter-Ideas — 61
Being Proactive — 61

DEFUSE THE DANGEROUS COUNTER-IDEA	62
THE DIRECT APPROACH©	64
THE REPLACEMENT APPROACH©	68
BENEFITS OF DEFUSING	71
CHOOSING THE "OTHER SIDE"	72

2. STAGE — 75

SURFING	76
2-A. WRITE YOUR THESIS STATEMENT	79
WHY WE HAVE THESIS STATEMENTS	79
LET THE IDEAS GUIDE THE THESIS	80
THE SINGLE-THOUGHT THESIS© TECHNIQUE	81
BE CONFIDENT	83
2-B. SEQUENCE OUR IDEAS	84
THE FLEXIBILITY OF THE T-VIEW OUTLINE©	84
SEQUENCING OPTIONS — TWO ROADS	85
HIERARCHY OF STRENGTH	86
BUILDING UPON PRIOR IDEAS	88
FOCUS ON THE BEST ARGUMENTS	90
THE IDEA STACK©	91
2-C. TIMING LADDER©	92
POSITIONING OURSELVES FOR SUCCESS	92
DIVIDE TIME INTO TWO BLOCKS	94
STAGING COMPLETE	100

3. WRITE — 101

STRATEGY MAP FOR WRITING OUR ESSAY:	102
3-A. WRITING MODELS	103
FIRST WRITING MODEL — THE DESIGN LAYER	109
PERSUASIVE COMMUNICATION BY DESIGN	109
THE DESIGN DEFINED	114
WRITING THE INTRODUCTION	116
SECOND WRITING MODEL — THE IDEA STACK© LAYER	117
WRITING FROM AN IDEA STACK©	118
FAST FOOD	119
ALL IDEAS ARE NOT CREATED EQUAL	121
THIRD WRITING MODEL — THE NAIL DOWN© LAYER	123
THE NAIL DOWN©	124
DESCRIBE OUR IDEA	125

PROVE OUR IDEA	127
TELL WHY IT IS IMPORTANT	129
THE THREE-LAYER MODEL© IS COMPLETE	132
WHEN TO WRITE WHAT GUIDE©	133
3-B. ENGAGE THE READER	134
HIT© - HOW TO PUT STYLE INTO THE INTRODUCTION	135
TITLE STRATEGIES	139
HOW TO PUT STYLE IN THE IDEA STACK©	140
HOW TO PUT STYLE IN THE CONCLUSION	145
READABILITY	146
3-C. LINKING WRITING WITH THE CLOCK	150
MAKING TIME WORK	150

4. CROSS THE GAP!   153

THE ONE THING	154
THE POWER TO PROVE EITHER SIDE	156
ROLL OVER, FLUFFY!	157
CATS RULE, DOGS DROOL	160
ANTICIPATE WHAT'S ON THE TEST	162
THE LAST CONCLUSION	165

5. REAL STUDENTS IN ACTION   169

WHAT'S HERE FOR YOU	169
I. WHAT ANCIENT ROME COULD TEACH ROMEO AND JULIET (T-VIEW OUTLINE©)	170
II. TASK FORCE (THE DESIGN – FIRST WRITING MODEL)	175
III. RISK (THE IDEA STACK© - SECOND WRITING MODEL)	179
IV. THE FUTURE OF SCIENCE (THE NAIL DOWN© – THIRD WRITING MODEL)	182
V. NEW AIRPORT IN CHICAGO (ENGAGING THE READER)	186

6. FUNCTIONAL INDEX   191

SYSTEM VIEWS	191
STRATEGY TOOLS	192
PERFORMANCE SECRETS	194
WRITING MODELS	198

Gratitude

When I started consulting with Oracle to develop an online school for grades K-12, I knew that the project was too expensive before Oracle figured that out and cancelled the entire project due to cost overruns. While I was consulting with Mobil Oil about how to deliver job skills to oil field workers when they performed dangerous tasks, I wished every student in America had a similar system to guide them through their schoolwork. It was then that I realized the way I got myself through school <u>was</u> <u>that</u> <u>similar</u> <u>system</u>, and the <u>book</u> in your hands <u>delivers</u> <u>it</u>.

The system didn't come to me over night. It came over years of watching and listening to parents, siblings, teachers and classmates – and then figuring out how to excel on the exams. As I reflect on all the talented individuals who coached, taught and invested in me, the following deserve special mention:

- **Mom**, who taught me to read fifty words by the time I was 18 months old
- **Dad**, for always believing I could do anything I put my mind to
- **Grandmother Frances**, who challenged me to think for myself
- **Eric Johansen**, my High School buddy, who got me to stop talking in class long enough to hear what my teachers were saying
- **Mrs. Doughberry,** my 7th grade teacher, who woke me up
- **Gustaf Gary Gillberg**, the inspiring Mr. G.G.G., my Algebra and Geometry teacher, who showed me how to make learning fun
- **George Morin**, my Trigonometry teacher, who taught me to be responsible for my own learning
- **Joseph Genereux**, my Physics teacher, who introduced me to using systematic approaches to solving problems
- **Jim Asnis,** team leader, who taught me executive communication skills
- **Dr. Brent Powell**, my manager, who trained me to communicate with many different kinds of people and develop training that worked
- **Rich French**, my manager, for his brilliant insights into skill assessment and classroom presentation
- **Dr. Rex Allen**, business leader, for tutoring me personally in Learning Theory and the science of Instructional Design
- **Linley**, **Cassandra**, **Karianne** and **Forrest,** my siblings, who provided honest and critical feedback on the various drafts of this book
- **Daniel**, my nephew, for sharing his powerful essay
- **Sidnee**, my niece, for sharing her perceptive essay
- **Benjamin**, my nephew, **Alora**, **Charisse**, **Elizabeth** and **Kiersten**, my nieces, for their patience during my test sessions
- **J.B. Simms**, for showing me the light at the end of the publishing tunnel
- **Deborah Kennedy**, for expertise on marketing this work
- **Madeline**, my daughter, for being the inspiration to finish this book

Quick Start – How to Write a High Scoring Essay

- Perhaps you are struggling to get the grades you want in school.

- Maybe you are doing well… but realize it gets harder each year.

- Some of you are the brightest student in your class and want to keep your edge.

- For each one of you, **this book delivers a solution!**

Your personal search to do better is real. The desire comes from **not knowing what** is **going on** in **school**. It has little to do with luck, your teacher or your intelligence. What is happening is that **both** teachers and students **think** that school is about **what** is being **taught** in class. **It is not**. Knowing the information your teachers teach and knowing what's in your textbook is **not enough** to **score well** on a test. You have to know **what to do** with it. This means that for you – school is about **performance**.

Performance is the game that is going on between teachers and students in school. This book reveals what is happening behind the scenes and how you can start playing that game – **to your advantage.**

As you learn to play the game of **Performance** in school, your worries about school will fade away, because you can now handle anything the teacher throws at you. One of the first performance skills someone probably taught you was how to cross a street without being run over.

I can still hear the words of my grandmother as she taught me to cross my first street safely. Now I will share those words with you and use them to illustrate the three key steps to **"Write a High Scoring Essay."**

The No-Study Solution! – Writing Essays

 When crossing the street, the first thing you do is **"don't step off the curb until you know the coast is clear."** If the coast is clear, you will probably make it across the street in one piece.

The first thing you do when writing an essay is **"don't start writing until you know what you are going to say."** You do this by jotting down a list of the points you plan to make. Then you look at your list and consider if the points build up to a consistent story. If not, you change your list before you start writing. When the list makes sense – you write. If the coast is not clear, you stay on the sidewalk. When the coast is clear, you step off. While the photo on the left shows <u>checking</u> to see if the <u>coast</u> is <u>clear</u>, the picture on the right shows <u>knowing</u> what you are going to say before you write.

Looking to see if the coast is clear   Seeing what you are going to write

While walking across the street, why is it so important that *"the coast is clear?"* It is important because we have only <u>one</u> <u>goal</u>: to cross the street safely. Being flattened by a car is bad. Getting to the other side without a scratch is good. Who has not heard this conversation or grasped the concept? Turn to **pages 33-35** to learn how to write this list of what you are going to say before you write it. In life, we teach that there is only one thing to focus on – crossing the street safely. In school, we teach that there is only <u>one</u> <u>goal</u> when writing an essay: to prove our **thesis statement**. For tips on how to write an engaging thesis statement and powerful examples of good and bad thesis statements, please turn to **pages 80-82**.

 When crossing the street, the second thing you do is **"keep looking both ways to spot oncoming traffic."** If you keep looking both ways, you will see the vehicles as they appear and avoid them.

Now that you have a list of things to say and a thesis to prove, the second thing you do is "***write a list that comes from the other direction."*** You do this by jotting down a list of what someone would say if they argued the other point of view from your thesis. Once in the street, if a car starts coming at you from the other direction – you get out of the way. If a point of view challenges your thesis, you defuse it. While the photo on the left shows a girl looking both ways, the Second List on the right shows what one would say believing the other point of view. To learn how to write the other view, turn to **pages 36-40.**

Looking both ways as you cross   **Looking at both sides of a thesis**

Why is it important that you **"keep looking both ways to spot oncoming traffic?"** It is important because we want to take the safest path to the other side and the path may change while we are crossing the street. We build the safest path for writing our essay by numbering each point we desire to say in the order we wish to say them (1,2,3…etc.), see **pages 84-89.** We number our First List after writing the Second List, to deal with the changes in our path due to the other point of view. Now you can stay on your path as you write because you avoided the oncoming traffic. To see how a student writes to look the other way and avoid oncoming traffic, read **pages 64-67.**

 When crossing the street, the third thing you do is **"don't stop until you get to the other side."** If you keep moving, taking the shortest safe route to the other side of the street, you will get there in one piece.

Don't stop until you get to the other side   **Don't stop until you write all three parts**

The way to keep moving and get to the other side of your essay is to write an essay in three parts. You open with an Introduction. You build your middle by describing your Ideas. You focus the reader's opinion with a Conclusion. Executing all three parts keeps you on track and assures that you complete a logical and convincing essay. We illustrate the three parts of an essay with the Yellow and Blue colored squares above. Turn to **page 114** for a complete description of the three parts. Examples of how we use them powerfully to communicate appear on **pages 112** and **176-178**.

The **Quick Start** guide presented here is a simple way to remember how to write a high scoring essay. Both crossing the street and writing essays are dangerous to the careless. Both have a beginning, middle and an end. For those who choose to read and follow this book, this analogy becomes a memory device while writing your essay. We have done the work of creating this memory device for you. All that remains for you to do is to remember the device in the following summary table:

	Crossing the Street	Writing an Essay	Pages
	Sidewalk / Street / Sidewalk	INTRODUCTION / YOUR IDEAS / CONCLUSION	
1	*"Don't step off the curb until you know the coast is clear."*	Make a list and see what you are going to write before you write it.	33-35, 80-82
2	*"Keep looking both ways to spot oncoming traffic."*	Make a list of what others would say if they argued for the other way, and address it.	36-40 84-89 64-67
3	*"Don't stop until you get to the other side."*	Write your essay in three parts: Introduction, Ideas and Conclusion.	114, 112, 173-175

This **"How-to"** chart is your GPS for knowing where you are in an essay. You can recall this in your moment of performance whether in school taking a test, at home writing a paper or writing the essay of your life for a scholarship, college application or graduate thesis.

PERFORMANCE SECRET #0: Use the 3 keys to crossing a street safely to remember the 3 keys to write an essay effectively.

Notes to the Reader

CHAPTERS – I numbered the chapters from negative numbers to positive numbers on purpose. The idea is to mirror the journey. We start out in school reacting to what is thrown our way until we decide enough is enough. Then we change by taking responsibility for our experience. The journey is from negative to positive, and so the chapter numbers follow the same pattern: -1, 0, 1, 2 and 3…etc.

PRONOUNS – The use of pronouns in the text alternates between male and female to eliminate reading "he or she" or "him and her" repetitively. A side benefit is avoiding the inaccurate "they" when the person is actually singular. The assignment is random; therefore, the author infers nothing by a bank robber being a "she" and a tough teacher being a "he", or vice versa.

PEOPLE – The stories in this book are all true and actually happened. I changed some of the people's names when their actions or words did not reflect favorably on their legacy.

-1. THE GAP

The Gap Between the Teacher and the Test

Now we step into the student's world. In this world, there is a space. The space is the gap between what we <u>think</u> we know and what the teacher <u>expects</u> us to know on the test.

The only tangible proof we have that the gap exists is our grades, but our gut tells us it is there. We sense <u>something</u> is wrong. Here is how it happens: We enter the gap when we leave the classroom. While in the gap, we study hard, do what the teacher suggested and feel good about our effort. Then we walk into the test, unaware that our preparation is not enough, especially for the essay questions.

The exam starts. Soon we hit a challenging essay question. Emotional and mental pandemonium breaks out. Then we take a breath, and we work through the uncertainty. Now, on a roll, we write frantically until time expires. Our paper is collected.

Time passes.

Eventually, our paper comes back with a grade lower than expected. We disagree with the grader's comments. Worse, their "corrections" seldom show us how to earn a better grade in the future. The only thing we have learned is what not to do on the question we just got – which we will never get again.

Stuck with an evaluation that appears more opinion than fact, we seek something concrete. We yearn for some way to prepare. We seek a way to attack essays every time with success. The problem is that we never seem to get a clear vision of how to do it. We are stuck in the Gap Between the Teacher and the Test!

All the talk in the classroom centers on what we need to learn and how to get it right. Few people talk about why these things are important, what makes them work and how we might use them. Even fewer people are telling us the best way to use it effectively on an essay test. Nobody gives us a bulletproof game plan we can use to earn high grades consistently. The entire testing experience appears to be a big secret that only the "smart people" know.

How do you take a test? What are your thought processes? What strategies do you use to maximize your chances of getting the answers right?

Do you formulate a game plan for each test? You should. Are you able to make your limited time, work? You can. Do you know how to present the information in a way that maximizes your chances of getting high grades? You will – if you keep reading.

Most teachers excel at telling us about the subject and directing us to the chapters in the text covered on the next test. **The missing art is how to learn so that we succeed on the test.** How do you prepare for an exam? How do you make the most of the talent you have? How do you make decisions about what to say, how to say it and when to say it? What strategy do you use to come up with your thesis? **The lack of answers to these questions creates the Gap Between the Teacher and the Test.**

This book delivers a bridge for crossing that gap. Knowing, Preparing and Performing are the three skills used to leap the gap – **not studying.** This book is a journey of discovery into **Knowing**, **Preparing** and **Performing**. Once these skills belong to you – you will never find yourself in the gap again!

Being Smart Enough

Many of us give up hope of being successful in school because we do not think we are smart enough. *"What is the point in trying?"* we ask. Well, it is important to look deeper into this myth, because first, it is not true, and second, as long as we believe it, the myth is true for us.

Sometime in the past, in some way or in some subject, many of us decided that we were *"not smart enough."* This decision was premature. School is not over yet. We do not know all the test-taking strategies available. Specifically, we have not read this book. Quitting before the game is over, before we even know what assistance is available, makes it impossible for us to know whether we are smart enough or not.

At one time, I was one of those people who gave up early. I was just getting by with B's and C's; moving on to the next grade, hoping it would all be over some day so I could get on with my life. I believed that smart students got good grades and not so smart students like me, got – not so good grades! I lived in this fantasyland into Junior High. Then, one day, quite by accident and to the utter surprise of my teacher, I was suddenly smart enough – even smart enough to embarrass the teacher. Here is how it happened:

The crack in the wall seems to get bigger every day. The cinder blocks do not even line up any more. Older kids say Paxton Center School sits on a landfill, an old dump, making the building unstable, which means the walls could come tumbling down at any time just like Jericho. I wonder, *"In which direction should I run when the walls collapse? Will the wall cave in or will the wall cave out? Hmmm..."*

"Oh, yeah! I'm in English class. Better pay attention! Then again, it probably won't matter because I am so bad at English."

Our annoying teacher is up there again at the front of the room telling us about another thing we never heard of.

"Funny sight. She needs to go on a diet."

The old woman is rambling now. I glance around looking to see who else is bored.

"Gee, what she says doesn't even make sense and the book they gave us is way too thick to explain anything."

I fan the pages of my open textbook in disgust.

*"Wow, I almost forgot! I brought **The Battle for Iwo Jima** in my backpack! Awesome... I can read that!"*

Now all I need to do is sneak the book into the bottom of my desk. I wait for her to turn around and face the chalkboard,

"She's turning now...Quick!"

I silently pull the library book from my backpack, open it to my bookmark and slide **The Battle for Iwo Jima** by Robert Leckie into the lower level of my desk. The rear is open, making a nice shelf for reading books. The front and sides of the desk are solid metal, blocking her view. I feel smug about how smart I am at this deception. I have read dozens of books in Mrs. Doughberry's class. While it appears that I am listening to the lecture, perhaps even following along in the textbook on my desktop, I am actually reading a book hidden on the lower level from the teacher's view.

"Back to reading. What a great story! The U.S. Marines are throwing hand grenades all over the place and taking out Japanese pillboxes by the dozens. The Marines are unstoppable – crawling

up the sand dunes under heavy fire. Every man is winning the Congressional Medal of Honor. Strongpoint after strongpoint falls to hand grenades and Browning Automatic Rifle fire. Smoke and dust drift in the breeze. This next attack is shaping up to be a classic... let's see, we're bringing up the flame thrower, got to clear out this pillbox on the right trying to pin us down. Soon we can take out the main bunker straight ahead. I see it all in my mind now. Pineapple-like grenade in his hand, the Squad Leader pulls the pin, and throws a strike through the narrow slot housing the Japanese machine gun. The gun flashes back in anger with a crrraaack, crraack, crack! Meanwhile, the grenade is rolling around inside the pillbox at the feet of the enemy soldiers. Ka-Boom! Smoke and debris billow out. I hear the Squad Leader yell, **"Let's go!"** *We are going over the top! That doesn't sound like my Squad Leader...*

"Mark Hopkins! <u>YOU</u> come up to the chalk board immediately!"

"Uh-Oh. That's Mrs. Doughberry!" She turns to the class and announces,

"Now I am going to show what happens to YOU PEOPLE when you don't pay attention in class!"

Mrs. Doughberry sees everything as herself vs. the world. She refers to any one, two or more of us as "you people." Her rather smug smile lets us all know that she has already proved her point! I walk down the aisle towards the chalkboard...doomed to disaster. At the end of her outreached hand is a piece of chalk.

"You go right up to that chalkboard, young man, and circle the gerund in that sentence."

I take the dusty stick of chalk. I turn to face the green board. The room becomes deathly silent. Sixty-four eyes lock on my position.

"No one will ever let me forget this. Hmmm... Well, this is the first time I have ever heard of whatever she was talking about. What did she call it? Can't remember. Oh well..."

I stare at the sentence. The teacher barks impatiently.

"Go on!"

I feel the world around me closing into a narrow tunnel and all goes silent. It's just me and the board now.

OK, I can see the subject, that's an easy call, a noun; I decide to cover it in my mind with a blue box. The verb is pretty clear, I never mess up on that, I cover that in my mind with a red box, all right, blank those out in my mind, they're just boxes now... moving on.. There is a familiar word; it is short – about four letters – must be an adjective or adverb; I cover that with a yellow box. I see another one of those, now I have two yellow boxes. Prepositions are gray. The only word left on the board with no box, is this one ending with "i-n-g." I have no box for this... Hmmm...

"Come on now, you don't have all day, young man."

The teacher's yell jolts me out of deep thought.

"Yikes! This is it."

I guide the dusty chalk; it catches and slides in an uneven circle around the strange word.

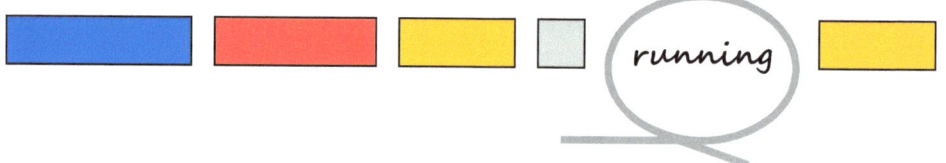

Now, I gently place the chalk in the tray and watch it settle into a bed of dust. A cloud of white powder floats in midair around my fingers.

All heads in the class turn towards Mrs. Doughberry to hear the verdict. I glance out of the corner of my eye, careful to avoid direct eye contact.

"Humph! Well, that _is_... the gerund. Return to your seat immediately!"

"Whew! Have I dodged a bullet!"

All student eyes follow me as I walk down the aisle, heads swiveling on their shoulders like a battleship's guns train on target. I'm looking into blank faces, then...

"There's a smirk, and a nod, and another smirk. I am a hero! Too bad they don't give out the Congressional Medal of Honor for this."

"Meanwhile, our teacher is lost in thought. She is regrouping. Her iron-fisted approach to discipline has backfired – I'm forcing her to change her approach to the lecture."

"In my seat now. The teacher has moved on, is writing more sentences on the chalkboard and she is looking for new victims. My heart is beating fast; it is thumping in my head. I feel it suddenly jump down slower. Wow. Soon a wave of calm flows over me – I am out of the action!"

"Now to survey the damage. Obviously, reading books is no longer an option in Mrs. Doughberry's class."

"What happened up there, anyway? How did I do that? It was just like playing Legos with those colored boxes in my head. I am not even close to the smartest kid in my grade, but I was smart enough up there – I out-thought the teacher! I bet I can do this again. I might even be able to get an A if I want to!"

Before this day, I thought school was all about knowing the answers by being smart; this meant to me that you had to be born smart to have any chance. I had given up hope of that long ago, but now, my experience with my colored boxes changed everything. I could out-think the teacher! A new world opened up, a world of thinking on my feet, being curious about how things work and challenging tests.

If you are like many students, you have wondered from time to time if you are smart enough to get good grades. Whether you believe it or not, **you already are smart enough.** How do I know that? Because being smart is the smallest part of doing well in school. Most of us know someone who is brilliant but does not apply himself. Based upon overall grades, he is not successful at school. Others, who do not seem that smart – do well. I think we could all agree, based upon these observations, that there must be more to doing well in school than being smart.

Students who succeed year after year, across all subjects, and on different kinds of tests, have a strong desire to prepare, develop their own strategies and adapt to new classroom situations. This book will show you how to do this, and soon you will be reacting to essay tests on your own in real-time. Then you will realize that you already are "smart enough."

It is Just a Card Game

People who play games learn the rules. They think constantly about how to use the rules to their advantage. Players know that if they can figure out strategies and make plays in different situations, they will win more often. We are going to look at the parallels between a card game and writing essays, and then pretend that answering an essay question is no bigger deal than playing a hand of cards. Adopting this attitude takes the stress out of taking a test.

In the weekends, holidays and vacations after my confrontation with Mrs. Doughberry, my family often played card games. I noticed that in every game we were either looking to score points or to avoid losing points. Meanwhile, whenever I approached a test in school, I either endeavored to get as many questions right as possible or attempted to avoid getting questions wrong. Tests and card games felt similar, and I realized that it was because in both situations, *someone was keeping score!*

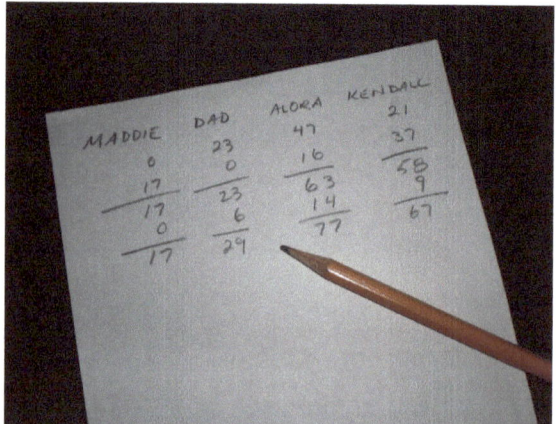

There was always a dealer, handing out cards. Once the dealer dealt, we picked up the unknown cards, and simply made the best choice we could when our turn came around. In a short time, the contest was over. We wrote down the scores and then started all over again with a new hand.

There are basic similarities between card games and tests. The teacher deals out sheets of paper, we pick up the unknown questions and we look to either get each question right or avoid getting each question wrong. We take our turn on each question. Each question is worth a specific number of points. When the test ends, the teacher calculates our point score.

While playing cards, our information is limited, 52 cards appearing in 4 different suits and 13 unique values. While taking tests our information is also limited: it is whatever chapters and topics we covered since the last test, unless of course this is a final exam. The teacher typically gives us a score of 0 to 100; a hand in a card game generates whatever score the game rules dictate. The game is over after a given number of hands. The test is over when time is up.

Every time we get to the next question on a test, we have to make a decision based upon what we are given; we choose an answer or write our thoughts down. In a card game, every time we get to our turn, we make a decision on what card to play out of the options in our hand.

As I started to see the similarities between playing a card game and taking a test, I saw that taking tests was no big deal; it was actually the same experience, just with different scenery. I began walking into tests with the attitude *"taking tests is just a game."* Tests became play. After all, my only goal was to score the most grade points. Every subject was the same now, because it was not about the subject at all, it was <u>about</u> <u>the</u> <u>game</u> – scoring points!

Now I was free to take on a test without stress, without thinking if I was going to be smart enough or not, without thinking if I was going to live or die, without thinking about my parents' reaction to my report card.

Being smart enough is a state of mind. I knew that in my moment of crisis in front of Mrs. Doughberry's class, it never occurred to me that I did not know the answer. I was just in the middle of a competition, reacting to what popped up in front of me, whether it was a machine gun opening up on the sands of Iwo Jima or a piece of chalk thrust into my hand with the command *"Circle the Gerund in that sentence."*

With my new attitude, school became one big game, I had a reason to be there, and I had a reason to pay attention. The subject did not matter; the teacher did not matter, because in the end, I would face a paper with information on it, play my cards, so to speak, and accept the score I earned. We seldom fret for long over a hand in cards; instead, we look forward to the next hand, the next chance to play better. I invite you to view taking tests as a game and to embrace the freedom and stress-free world it creates for you.

The Winning Attitude

Success in school depends upon your strategy and attitude. Many students think that all it takes to get high grades is to learn what is being taught in class – such as how to solve a quadratic equation in algebra – but learning is not enough. You must show up for school every day with the frame of mind that you are stepping on to the field for the big game or that you are walking down the runway in the big fashion show. Your actual big game or big show is the competition for grades in school.

This section gives you a way to keep the winning attitude alive each day. The approach is to take the winning attitude we have about one part of our lives and to transfer it to our school attitude. We start by looking at what our interests are right now, such as:

Sports

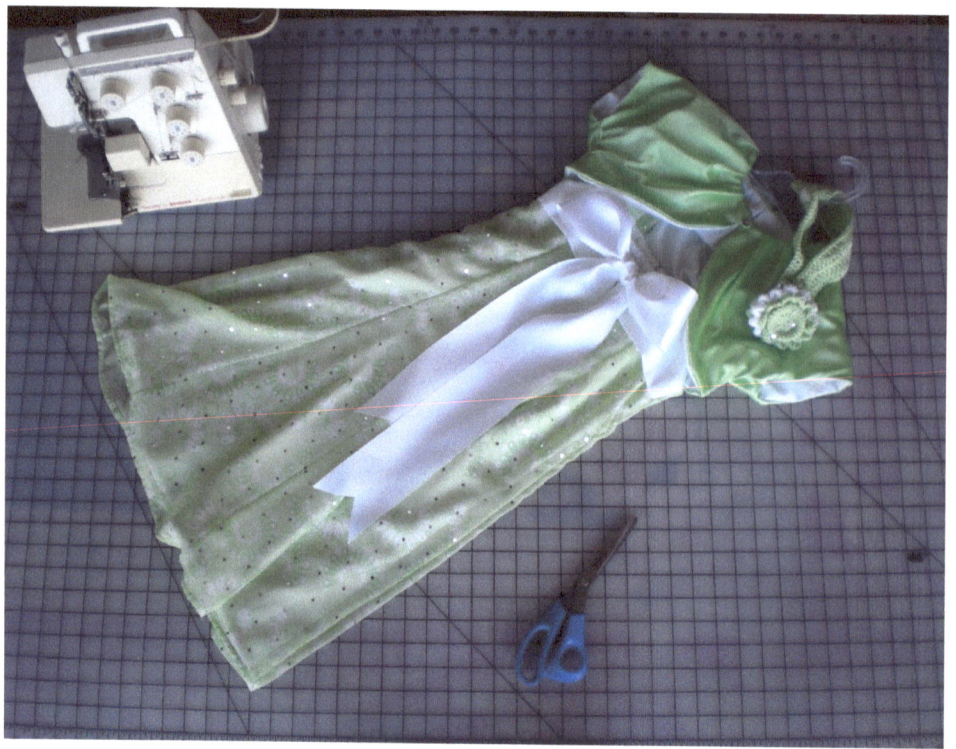

Fashion Design

High Adventure

Each of us is already excited about something. Many of us love sports, others fashion, it is hard to find anyone who does not enjoy music and most of us dream about being rich or having the perfect career when we grow up. Most of us probably already have a great attitude because we are reading this book to improve ourselves.

A powerful way to gain the winning attitude in any moment is to pretend that you are doing the thing you love the most – right before you start listening in class, preparing for an exam or taking a test.

One way to practice this skill is to see in your mind, feel in your heart and hear your thoughts as if you were doing what you love – right now. Then you shift instantly to your class, preparation or exam, and **decide** **this** **is** **part** **of** **it** while you still feel good. We now feel warm and fuzzy about school. Great athletes have won games or medals when they were sick or injured. Legendary performances such as these remind us that people can change the way they feel and perform at a high level whenever they choose. We are no different. The following diagram provides a visual representation of this method:

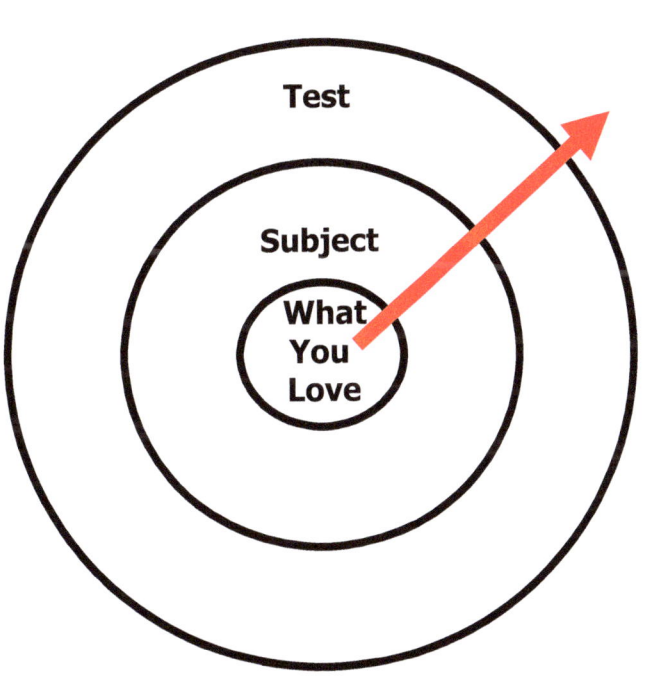

Our attitude affects every aspect of the learning experience, which effects how we do on every question on each test. This link between your attitude and your performance begins to show the truth behind the book's title – your success does not depend entirely upon how hard you study. It first <u>depends upon your attitude</u>.

A winning attitude opens up new doors of success. We feel differently about school. When we love something, we can handle its challenges and we want to know more about it.

Our attitude is the number one factor in the grades we receive. Imagine if we walked through Nordstrom's during the biggest sale of the year and were so preoccupied with why our dog did not play fetch today that we did not realize there was a sale going on. Many of us go through school like this – completely distracted.

How you eventually get to the point where you have fun taking tests and enjoy the game – does not matter. What is important is to _love_ the _game_ to the extent that you are fully engaged in the process of grasping information, presenting knowledge and scoring the most points.

When we come to school with the attitude to play the game to win, every moment in the classroom becomes an opportunity. The opportunity is to discover something that will be worth a few more points in the next game (taking the test). We _look forward_ to the _next test_ because that is _the only time_ we get to _play the game_!

> **PERFORMANCE SECRET #1: View taking tests as playing a game. Love playing that game.**

0. THE SYSTEM

Game Plan

Every champion comes to the game with a plan to win. We may not be athletes or card sharks, but we still approach everyday life with a plan. Whether we are organizing Friday night out with our friends or strategizing how to find the perfect outfit, we create a plan because we know it improves our chances of success. So why then, with something that has a far greater impact on our future, do we walk into a classroom bringing nothing more than a vague idea of what we are going to do? Why would we put someone else in control of the situation? Why wouldn't we plan this out as thoroughly as we do our fun? It just makes more sense for us to be in charge rather than them... Right?

This book delivers a system that puts you back in control of the classroom situation. We can now walk into our test with a complete plan, one proven by students who used it to achieve A's at first-rate schools in America. Some of their essays and techniques appear in Section "5. REAL STUDENTS IN ACTION."

This proven plan has three phases: the **THINK** phase, the **STAGE** phase and the **WRITE** phase.

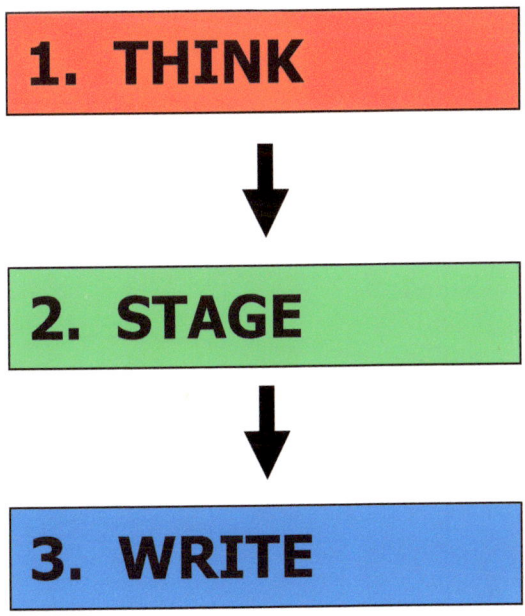

Think, Stage, Write is the process we use to handle essay questions. The simple three-phase approach changes our game. We now walk into the exam knowing exactly what is going to happen. As we execute our own plan, we experience being in control. This execution gives us confidence. A confident student who thinks will be successful. This is exactly who we want to be.

> **STRATEGY TOOL #1: Walk into the exam with a game plan:**
>   1st – Think
>   2nd – Stage
>   3rd – Write

The Elements

In our game, instead of interacting with a ball (as happens in most sports) we interact with three elements:
1. **Information**
2. **Location**
3. **Time**

These elements are as concrete in our learning world as a basketball and hardwood floor are in the athletic world. **Information** includes the idea we want to prove, the argument we will present to prove it, and the facts, data and logic we use to back up those arguments. **Location** is choosing where and when to present the Information. **Time** is the minutes the teacher gives us and becomes the balancing factor for choosing Information and Location.

Obviously, when we are writing an essay without time constraints, the time element is not a big factor. Writings in this category include critiques, research papers and take-home exams. Those instances aside, we maximize our grade by <u>balancing</u> Information and Location <u>across</u> Time. Our mind blends these three ingredients together in real time as we write or type an essay. A triangle illustrates the interdependence of these three elements. Throughout the book, we will expand our understanding of these elements until we have models, strategies and tools we can use to achieve higher grades.

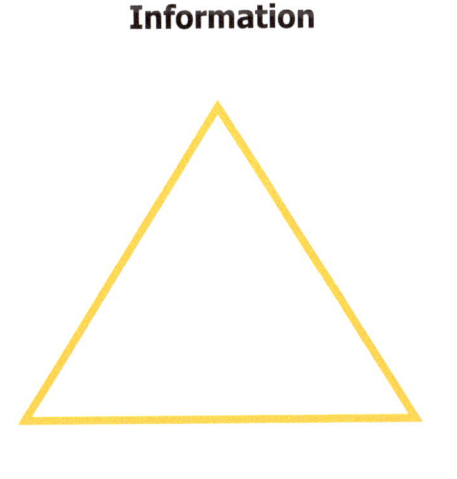

The System Revealed

When we blend our game plan with the elements, we get the complete performance system shown below. This is our first look, so there is no need to grasp it all now; that is the purpose of this book. Simply be open to the possibility that you have found a system and that it will bring you success.

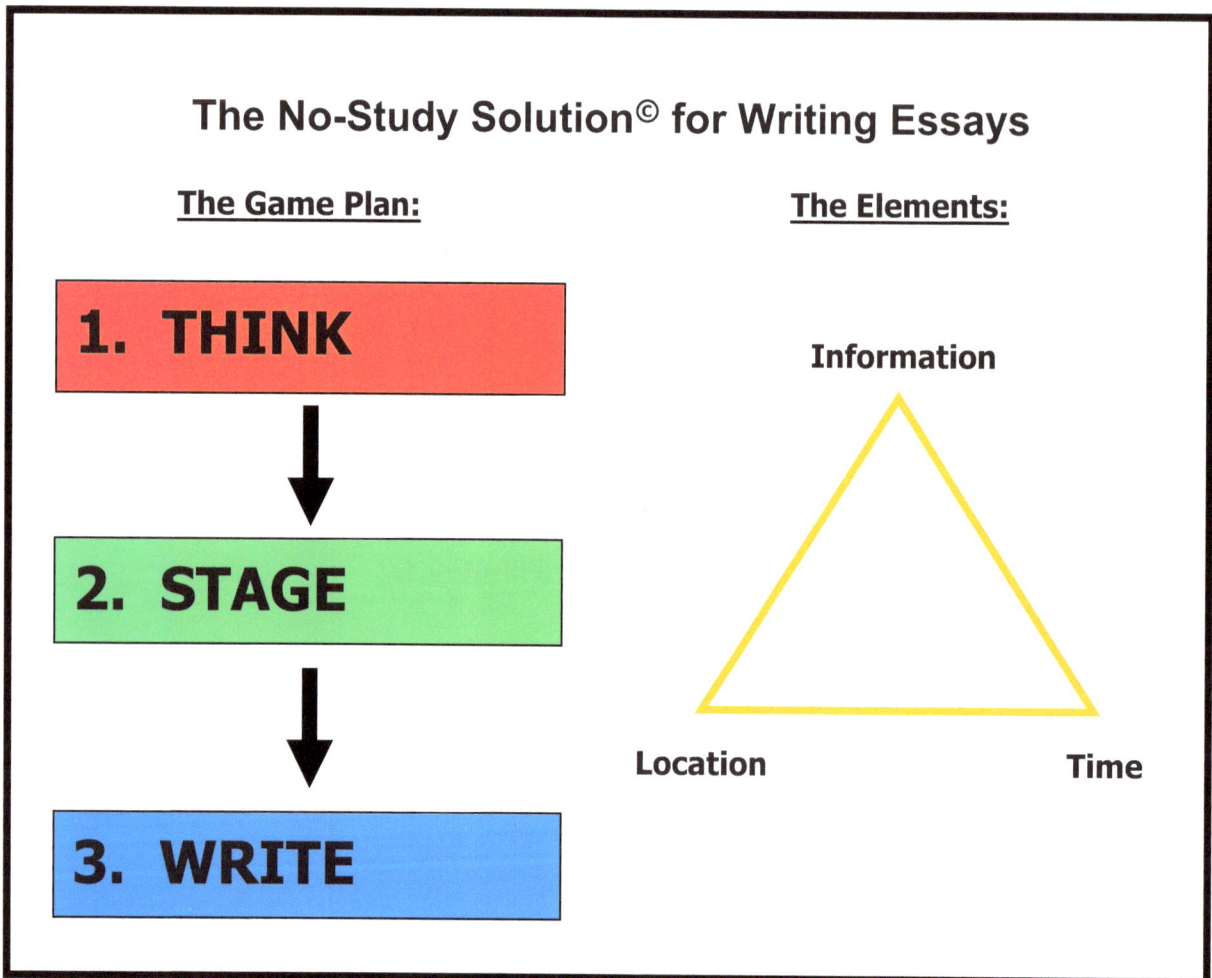

Just remember that every aspect of **The No-Study Solution**© comes in threes and it will prompt you to remember each piece. It is as easy as one-two-three. Now, we will bring this system to life as I share how I used it to answer an essay question on my final exam in graduate school and score an A.

THE ONE SYSTEM: The No-Study Solution© for Writing Essays

Real Life Situation

When we take a system to its extreme limits in the classroom, we find out how well it works and how far we can take it. What better limit to use than the University of Chicago, Graduate School of Business, ranked 4th at the time of this situation? Here high entrance requirements fill the class with the brightest students and these students ensure there is competition for the few A's available. What better grader to benchmark the score I will receive on my essay than Dr. Walter Fackler, once Senior Economist for President Dwight D. Eisenhower's Cabinet Committee, now Associate Dean as well as my professor? His experience testifying before congressional committees and consulting with business, government agencies and foundations will be a real-world test of my written communication strategies and approach.

As I faced this scenario, the challenge for me personally was that based upon past academic performance, I did not stack up well against my competition. My GMAT test score and college GPA were at the bottom 10% of those accepted into the program. In this class, there are 90 students graded on a curve, and the majority of them are full-time students, while I split my time between a full-time day job and part-time night school.

Although they are out of sight a few floors below me, I am reminded that thousands of Christmas Shoppers are swarming the high-end shops along the street below, looking for the ultimate Christmas gift, while I am spending the next three hours of my life taxing my brain in this final exam. Wow. What a contrast. It is 6:29 pm. Here comes Dr. Fackler. He announces, "The exam has begun!" He is handing out the instructions and blue essay booklet.

As I scan the instructions, I see there are suggested times for each section; there is a potpourri of question types... fill in the blank, problems and essays. Wow, this last essay is 45 minutes! Knowing that three hours will pass quickly, I start answering questions and calculating math problems. Before long, I arrive at the 45-minute essay question asking me to provide advice to the Mayor on where to build another airport in Chicago. My classmates are frantically writing away, desperately attempting to beat the clock. However, I drift into deep thought ... "How can I get an "A" against this competition?"

If I do not approach this essay in a radically different way from what I have always done, I am going to end up at the bottom of the grade scale. That will be not only embarrassing but also expensive. My employer IBM will only reimburse my tuition if I score a B+ or higher. I'll definitely have to do something different.

Everybody around me knows his or her stuff. Everyone is highly motivated. Everyone else in my class is one of the "smart people." Where can I get an advantage?

With a superior strategy, that's where! I have always written as much as I could, as fast as I could, putting down as many big words as I could find. I wonder how many students around me are doing that? This is how everybody does it, right?

Well, maybe not. What have I learned over the past 5 years at IBM about talking to business executives? If I put the marketing, sales, and presentation skills that I have learned in the business world to work producing an essay, I will write an essay that is so clear and powerful; Dr. Fackler will have to give me a high score. I will anticipate that the other "smart people" will use the old strategy of writing maximum volume, giving me a chance to shine! I will use my communication skills to score a few more points than the others will. Thanks to the Grade Curve, that is all I need – a slight advantage.

So, how do I make this a reality? I will get into Dr. Fackler's world. What is his experience going to be grading my essay? Will he be tired of reading wordy responses by the time he gets to my paper? Yes. Will most of the students recommend the same solution for the same reasons? Yes. He may even get bored reading the same approach. I realize that originality will be a key advantage.

I have to make sure he knows that I understand the deep meaning of the key principles of the course. Dr. Fackler really cares about economics. Caring will hit him on an emotional level as well as intellectual level. Lastly, he probably has a checklist of terms he is looking for me to explain in the essay. I need to hit each one. I want him to check off all the items on his list... hmmm, maybe a table of some sort comparing the airport locations.

I can grab his attention by how my essay is structured, the way I lay out my information and how he feels reading it. Remember, he will be reading 90 essays. If I could get all the information in a clearer more compact format than the others, I will overcome the fatigue factor and be refreshing. I will use precision over volume, and to do that, I will need to write from a detailed outline.

While I am focused on the feel of my essay, given that this is a business school, why not write in the style of business? What would that be? Let's see... The Wall Street Journal – of course! How do they do it? The Wall Street Journal typically begins a business article with a person's story who is affected by the news in the article – to grab the reader emotionally. I will make my first sentence grab Dr. Fackler the way an article in the Wall Street Journal grabs. He will be interested.

My language will sound straight to the point, the way Dr. Fackler would advise President Eisenhower. I want to complete an area and then move on to the next with no loose ends, the way an expert would do it, again, another reason for an outline covering all the key points of the course. I want my thoughts to be clear and move with velocity. I need to look prepared and like an advisor, so I will build a presentation table that connects the location options to all the key decision factors that go into where to put the airport. I'll place the table in the conclusion to save time. That way, I will not lose any grade points for missing some item on Fackler's list I neglected to mention. This is the way experts advise business leaders – hit the high points and include the details in the white paper. He will hear an expert talking.

The speed of thought is much faster than the speed of reading. The story I shared above comes across in slow motion. In reality, it took only seconds to envision in thought. This approach had far-reaching implications on how I used my 45 minutes. Now, instead of starting to write, and thinking as I went, I spent 20 minutes building a detailed outline and summary table. Then I shifted to writing my essay for the remaining 25 minutes. I laid down my facts with laser crispness from the outline and completed my essay with time to spare. Remember, I am writing to a man who has advised the President of the United States. He knows how it is done and expects the same. The results were extraordinary, as extraordinary as an A can be, and a copy of the graded essay now appears as **New Airport in Chicago**, page 187-188.

Be Teacher-Focused

On the cover of this book, we introduced the idea of getting higher grades without studying. Students usually study to memorize information for a test. In the real life experience above, the student used different strategies to jump his performance far above his normal ability. He did not "study" harder. Being in the bottom 10% typically scores a D, or 60-69 points. A student in the top 10% scores 95 points on average, or an A. By using the techniques in this book, the student raised his grade at least twenty-six points (95-69=26 points). This is the power behind using **The No-Study Solution**©'s concepts.

A smart person may not always perform in a smart way. Each of us has an opportunity to stand out from the crowd by thinking first, organizing our information second, and writing solid arguments third. A student who is smarter than we are may be able to remember all the information required better than we can; however, he may be in too big of a hurry to present it an interesting and persuasive way. An impressive essay is one that shows we not only know the answer, we have the skill to present it in a clear, concise and engaging manner.

If we consider the teachers' experience when correcting our essay, we realize that the best way to annoy her is to show that we do not care. With this insight, showing that we care becomes a top priority in designing our response. We start by caring about her problem of correcting our exam. People who have thought about something long enough to get to the essence of it, care about it. Clear and short communication conveys both messages. As described in the last section, writing from an outline made it possible to earn an A while only using 25 of the 45 minutes allotted for the question. A short essay made Dr. Fackler's job of correcting my paper easier because the key points stood out. Dr. Fackler and most teachers really care that we learn the significance of what they teach. Teachers want to know that we learned not only <u>what</u>, but also, <u>how</u> and <u>why</u>. The best way to show that we learned what our teacher cares about is to write a well thought-out essay.

Additionally, people who care, take the time to make sure others do not waste time interacting with them. I know Dr. Fackler appreciated reading my essay because he <u>underscored</u> the "A" grade <u>with</u> <u>a</u> <u>smile</u> – not the typical reaction of a professor. I had done his work for him by summarizing the key principles and facts on a single page – just in case he missed something. When we anticipate the list of items that our teacher requires for full credit, we make our teacher's job easy. We give him what he is looking for. On an emotional level, we are communicating to him that we cared about his class and that he did a "good job" teaching us. We focused on his needs. This is being Teacher-Focused.

Eliminating Stress

It is normal to feel stress when our performance is being graded critically – such as when taking a test. Emotions play a decisive role in our ability to perform, and consequently, the grades we can achieve are often affected more by our stress level than by our intelligence or genetics. I recall reading the university newspaper one day when a credible source revealed that our starting quarterback cared so much about doing well that he threw up before every football game. Yet, years later, he retired from professional football having had a rewarding and fruitful career. Whatever anxiety he had was obviously not a deterrent to being successful.

To perform well in school, it is highly beneficial to realize where our anxiety comes from. Are we concerned that every aspect of our performance is graded? Are we concerned about what our classmates will think of us if they see our grade? Do we compare our grades to those of our brothers and sisters? Are we allowing grades to determine our self-worth?

Our stress over tests usually comes from believing that our grade says something about who we are. If we get a high grade, we are smart and successful. If we get a bad grade, we are stupid and a loser. This logic is defective. We are who we are regardless of the grade we achieve. Meanwhile, how successful we ultimately are depends upon the extent to which we <u>Know</u>, <u>Prepare</u> and <u>Perform</u>.

Knowing is replacing self-doubt with the plan – **THINK**, **STAGE**, **WRITE**. With this strategy, we always know where we are in the process, what to do at each moment, and when we are done. We have confidence because we are in control and following our own game plan. We replace anxiety with confidence.

Preparing includes using what is in this book and observing our results. We learn a new technique, use it on the next test and observe the result. We evaluate its effectiveness. Then we use it again and perhaps tweak it a little bit. Once the strategy or technique is working for us, we claim victory. Now we look for the next tool to plug into our game plan. The preparation is similar to how an excellent athlete uses video to slow down her movements in order to spot what she is doing. Once the physical movement is isolated, she corrects and perfects her technique by making an adjustment in practice. Then the athlete uses the adjustment in competition. The result is a boost in her performance.

As we learn to love the game of taking tests, we get lost in the fun. Stress and anxiety fade away, replaced by our love to play the game. As we focus on the game, we are in the "eye of the storm" – calm, alert and focused – a top performer!

1. THINK

> **1. THINK:**
>   **1-A. Think Up Ideas**
>   **1-B. De-Bug Ideas**
>   **1-C. Defuse Counter Ideas**

In this section, you will learn the secrets to:
- *Create and organize the best ideas*
- *Gain deeper insight*
- *Avoid being victimized by trick questions*
- *Subtly discredit opposing views*

Thinking is the first step in our 3-step process for writing essays. Our Game Plan is THINK – STAGE – WRITE. Thinking is the one-step most students overlook. Surprisingly, many students believe that they are Thinking when in reality they are not. At one time, the most successful company in America was IBM, and Tom Watson their founder displayed one plaque on his desk, and on it appeared a single word…"**THINK**". Obviously, Tom had some extremely bright people working for him, yet every day his #1 focus was to remind his people to think. Thinking has a positive impact on any endeavor of excellence. Given the significant extent to which thinking can improve our grades, we focus this entire section on what it means to think.

1-A How to Think up the Ideas

The Mind Scores more Points than the Pen

How and when do we create and organize our ideas? Many students think things up as they write and create a fragmented essay. They are the "write on the fly" crowd. Others write down everything related to the subject they can remember in order to hit what the teacher is looking for. These folks are the "shotgun" crowd.

> ***"I didn't have time to write a short letter, so I wrote a long one instead."*** – Mark Twain

Both the "write on the fly" and "shotgun" approaches are obsolete. Yes, they are popular, but popularity does not make them the best strategy or even a good strategy. These popular approaches fail on two levels: first, an essay question tests our ability to communicate clearly; and second, someone has to read it. The graders, who are reading our essays, do not enjoy random and meandering arguments. Neither do they like sifting through a chaotic avalanche of information to find out if we answered the question – or worse, what we really meant. These popular strategies make us look like we do not understand what is being taught in class. The result is that we get lower grades even when we know the material and have "studied hard".

The smart strategy is to know exactly where you are going and how you will express each idea – before you start writing. With this strategy, you are clear and precise with your writing.

The Second Draft is Always Better

Imagine that we have a time machine or magic wand that alters reality. Imagine using this device to fast-forward though our brain while we are writing our essay. We could then extract all the brilliant thoughts, capture remembered facts, and observe the results of the essay we wrote. Now, by going to the future, we can see what we wished we could have changed, left out, or said in a different way if we had written the essay – even before we write the essay. With this imaginary device, we will write a better essay on the second pass, and with the magic wand, make it our first pass. This magic time machine is necessary because we do not have time to write two drafts in a real test situation. In the next few pages, I will show how to create such a device.

PERFORMANCE SECRET #2: The first action to take when writing an essay is not to write anything at all. The first action is to THINK.

Our reality-altering device uses our mind and organizes our thoughts on paper. This is not just any organization; it is a STRATEGY TOOL designed to capture our mind's imagination near the speed of thought. The first action we ever take to answer an essay question is to pause and think. We let the ideas flow through our mind, sort them into the best order, and visualize how the essay will look, sound and feel. We now reveal how this works.

The Power of Thinking on Paper

Where do we find our reality-altering device? We start with a piece of paper. Being opportunistic, we find this anywhere we can, the back page of the test, part of a handout or scrap piece of paper. First, we write down all of the ideas we want to say. We place these in a stack. (see picture below)

We are going to use a specific example to illustrate strategies and tools throughout the book. Starting now, we will refer to a hypothetical essay question, **Dogs vs. Cats**:

> **Consider the relative value of a cat verses a dog as a pet. Which pet generates the most value to both the pet owner individually and society as a whole?**

Each of us may have a preference. We may prefer a Dog to a Cat, or vice versa. For the purposes of our dialogue, let us assume we prefer dogs. Now back to making our list, we write down all the positive ideas for dogs. After a minute or so of thinking, we have generated the following list:

- WORK
- SIGHT DOGS
- POLICE K-9
- BITE THIEVES
- RACING
- PLAY CATCH
- PROTECT FAMILY
- LIVE 10-14 YEARS
- HANG OUT
- WALK 2x A DAY
- TRAINABLE
- BARK LOUD

We are calling this a list of <u>ideas</u> in the text rather than list of <u>points</u> to be made or list of <u>reasons</u> because behind each word is a robust idea why this word is important. Explaining "<u>the</u> <u>why</u>" is where we earn a higher grade. The word *RACING* stands for the <u>idea</u> that Greyhounds and Whippets chase a mechanical rabbit around an oval track. The dogs wear large numbers on small "aprons" flanking their sides. People in the stands can see the dogs as they circle the track. The large numbers on the animal's sides make it easy for the people to watch their dog throughout the race. Spectators often bet money guessing which dog will win. An entire industry revolves around the breeding and training of dogs and the operation of racetracks. This one word in our list, *RACING*, is a placeholder for everything about Dog Racing. There is no reason to write down more detail than the word *RACING*. We keep it as brief as possible so we can work with the idea, *RACING*, rather than clutter things up with lots of information. After all, the reason *RACING* is even listed on our T-View Outline©, is that we believe *RACING* demonstrates that dogs deliver more value than cats. Have you ever seen a cat race?

If you are curious how it all turns out, visit the "Dog is Better" essay **Roll Over, Fluffy!** starting on page 157. To read an essay written from the other side, read the "Cat is Better" essay **Cats Rule, Dogs Drool**, pages 160-161. Between here and there, we will discover exactly how to build a high scoring essay. We begin by mastering our time altering device, the T-View Outline©.

The T-View Outline©

Now we add a sifting tool to our list. This STRATEGY TOOL is simply two straight lines drawn at right angles to each other in such a way that they form the letter "**t**". The structure of this shape organizes our ideas. The benefit is that we can get a forecast of the dog essay on the left and a forecast of the cat essay on the right – in seconds. (Think time altering device) Writing both essays becomes unnecessary. By seeing each essay in idea form, we will be able to choose the stronger essay before we write it. Named for its shape, we simply call this the **T-View Outline©**.

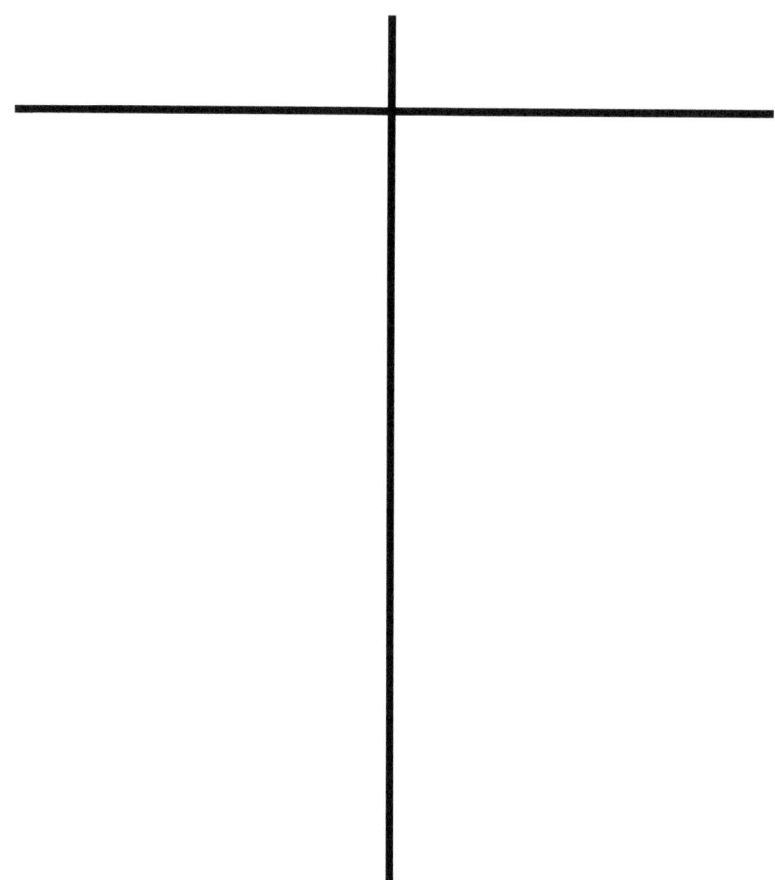

The T-View Outline© gives us a view into the future by comparing the pros and cons of both sides of a question before we expend a lot of physical energy and time writing an essay.

We draw the T-View Outline© above and to the right of our list of ideas so that the list ends up in the bottom left hand corner of our STRATEGY TOOL.

```
— WORK
— SIGHT DOGS
— POLICE K-9
— BITE THIEVES
— RACING
— PLAY CATCH
— PROTECT FAMILY
— LIVE 10-14 YEARS
— HANG OUT
— WALK 2x A DAY
— TRAINABLE
— BARK LOUD
```

These are free and creative moments for us as we write down all angles, ideas, details and facts we can think of that would prove the viewpoint that dogs are the most valuable pet. There is no risk right now, because nothing is permanent. We are fast-forwarding in time to see what our essay will look like. Our thoughts are fluid and we will play around with them as we build a solid outline.

The No-Study Solution! – Writing Essays

As we generate our list of unique ideas, we are capturing them close to the speed of thought. We jot down a few words or symbols to capture the idea; then we go to the next line and write down the next thought.

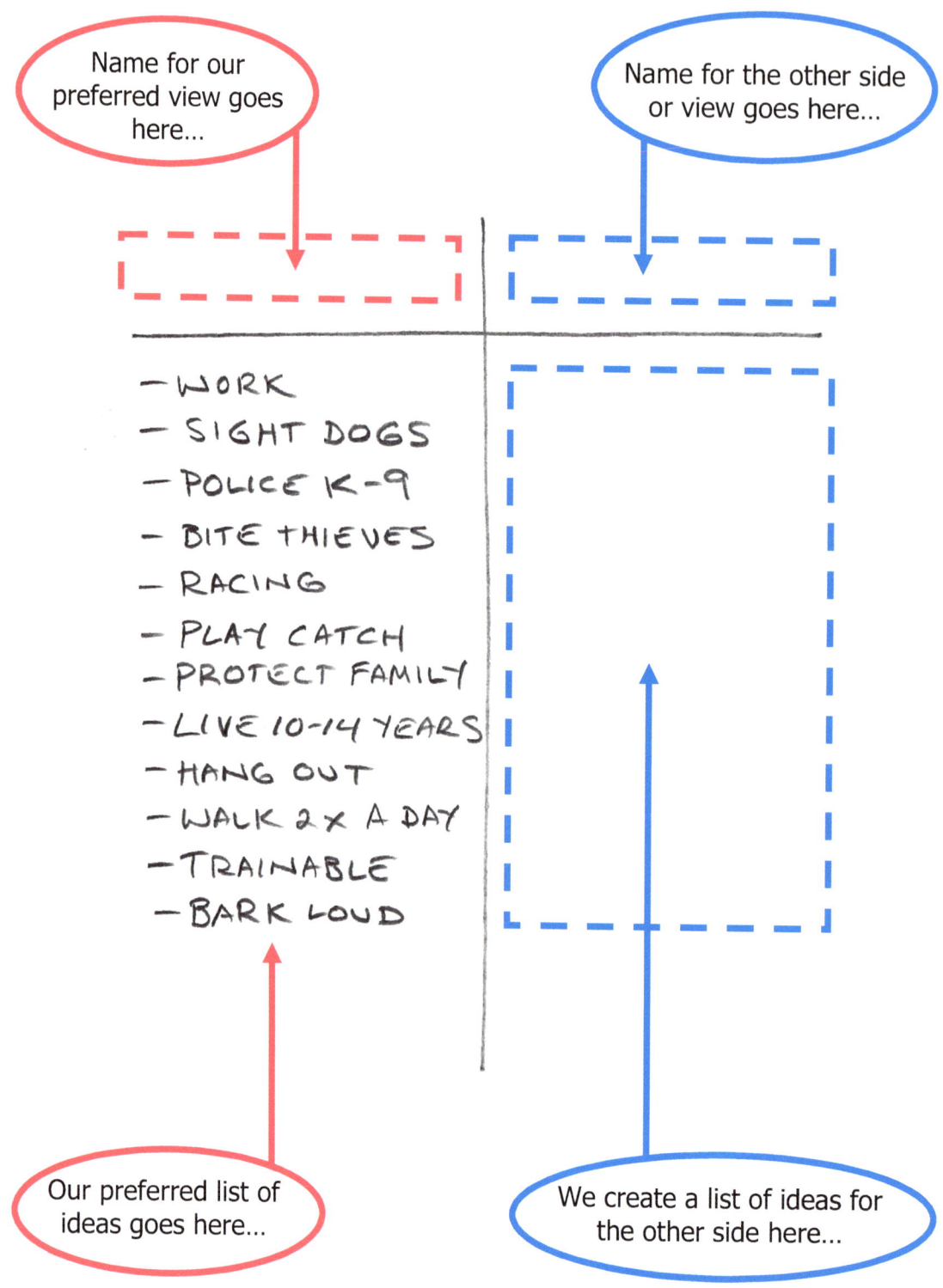

Once we have captured our initial bundle of thoughts, we jump over to the right side of the vertical line. Now we jot down a list of reasons why cats deliver more value. Our goal is to create this list with the same passion and honesty with which we created the list for "Viewpoint Dogs." Otherwise, we will not end up with a true measure of the strength of the Cat essay.

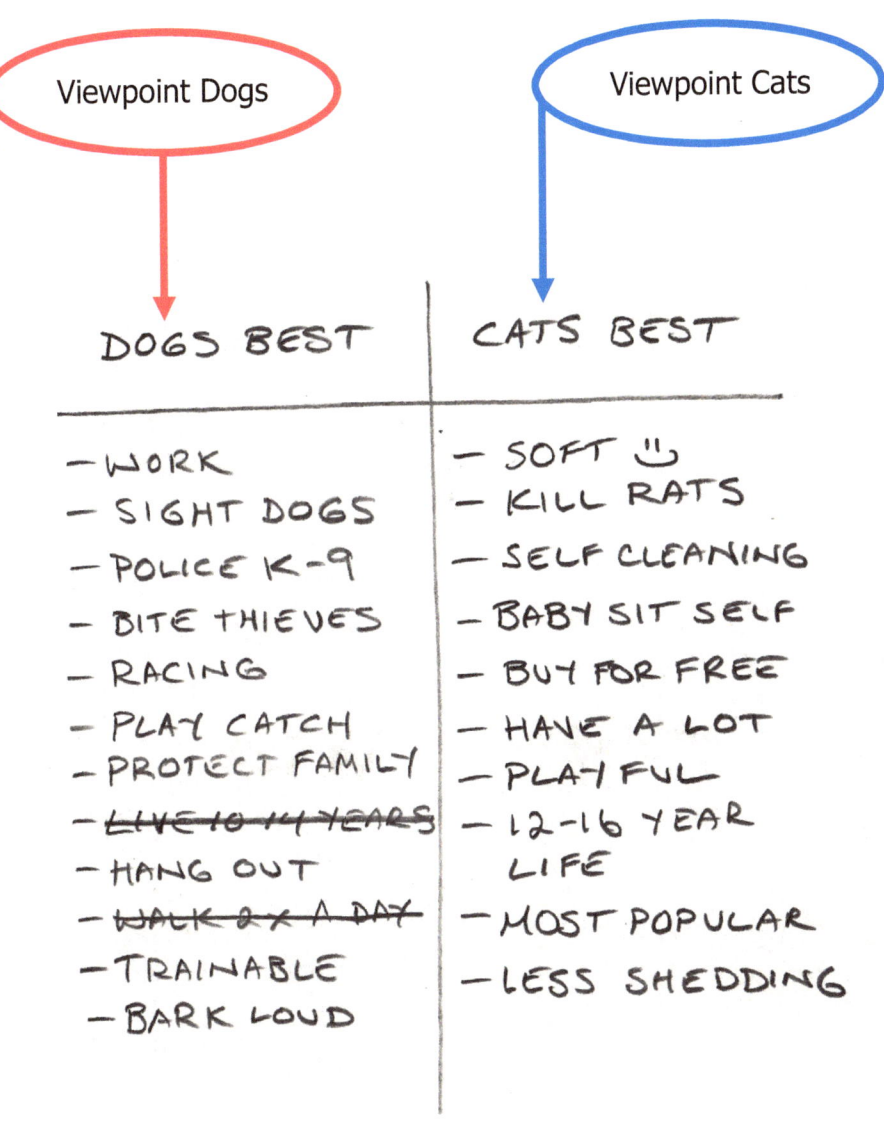

You don't want to lose any of those fleeting thoughts that come to you, so record them in the T-View Outline© in the shortest form that you will recognize: with a word, abbreviation or symbol. Then move on to the next insight as it flows through your brain. Allow your mind to race at full speed capturing the ideas with a word or two, leaving the descriptive words out until you actually write the essay.

There is no need to worry about how good the ideas are or even where they will go, simply capture them as quickly as possible. We will refine this list later. The goal right now is to draft two outlines of ideas, one to prove ***Dogs*** are more valuable and the other to prove ***Cats*** are more valuable.

> **STRATEGY TOOL #2:** Use the T-View Outline© to capture the best ideas, outline the essay and see both sides of an issue.

The T-View Outline© compresses time and opens up our mind to see both sides of the essay as a complete picture. We are not yet 100% sure which view provides the best chance of a higher grade. Soon we will learn to spot weaknesses in our essay, strengthen them and choose the higher scoring viewpoint before writing. Once a side is chosen, the T-View Outline© becomes our cue card from which we write.

On the back cover, I promised to give you the teachers' playbook by knowing what the teacher wants you to say. The T-View Outline© reveals what the teacher sees. On the preceding page, within the gray shaded square, is displayed a simplified summary of the reasons dogs are best and the reasons cats are best. The teacher will read many essays from both sides of the vertical line. Because the teacher reads and corrects many papers, he sees the question as displayed by this T-View Outline©. Since our goal is to position our paper to achieve the most favorable grade, it is highly beneficial to see both points of view. We will show you throughout the book how to write not only the most convincing pro-dog essay, but also one that out performs the pro-cat argument. Using the same techniques, a student could write a superb "Cat is Better" essay, see **Cats Rule, Dogs Drool** on pages 160-161. Starting now, we think from the teacher's two-view perspective; we play <u>in</u> their game, we play <u>on</u> their home field, we play <u>against</u> a team that is <u>both</u> opponent and umpire – and yet, despite the overwhelming odds – we win.

Personalize with Sight, Sound and Touch

Now that we have the T-View Outline© to play with, we will reflect on why this works. The tool works because it engages our key senses simultaneously. Our learning and thinking become more effective when each of our major senses: Sight, Sound and Touch are involved – a person has to both draw and look to create a T-View Outline©. Ideally, we would use cursive on our outline because it engages more of our brain. However, for clarity's sake, I chose to print each T-View Outline© in this book by hand. Meanwhile, you are the only person reading your outline and as long as you can read your own handwriting, cursive is ideal.

Senses are the human equivalent of computer input devices, such as scanners, optical character readers, keyboards and touch screens. Drawing a parallel, each of our senses records information differently. Those of us who are not aware of how we use each of own senses, miss the opportunity to maximize learning what is being taught in school. We can learn much about ourselves by observing our thoughts, watching our eyes and feeling our hands as we work with The T-View Outline©. Consider the following senses for a moment:

- **Sight**
- **Sound**
- **Touch**

Consider that we engage all of these senses when jotting down ideas in a T-View Outline©. Touch is engaged as we write. Sight is engaged as we observe the ideas flowing onto paper. Sound is engaged as we hear ourselves think. When we know how to use the sense we are best at, we learn more.

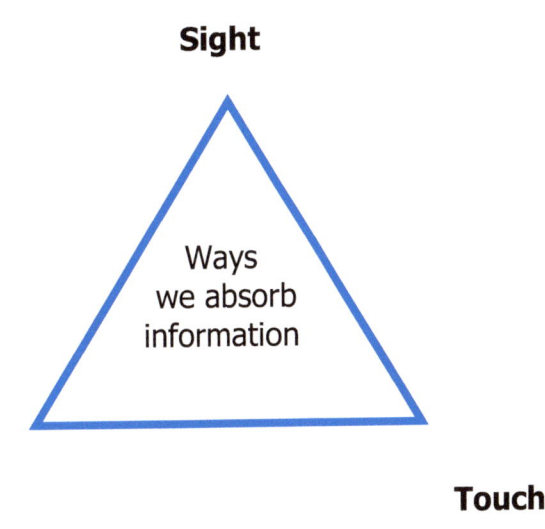

- **Sight** – If this is your primary learning sense, you enjoy drawing pictures. You probably write as you speak. You take a strong interest in visual appearance, how objects clash or go together. Many of you can remember pictures and pages in your mind. The key advantage for you is that when you draw while you are learning, you remember more deeply what you study. Taking notes is powerful for you. When using the T-View Outline©, take the extra time to draw the T and write in the headings. Your mind will process the entire picture at once and see the relationships between the two sides of an issue.

- **Sound** – If this is your primary learning sense, you most likely can quote the lines in a movie days after you saw it. You may not have considered that you can also play back the sound of your teacher's voice in your mind. This is a powerful key to your learning. It is strongly suggested that you consider tape recording your lectures and playing these back on your iPod as you go throughout your day. This one strategy may eliminate most of the studying you are doing because; once the sound tracks are "stored" in your brain, you can simply play them back in your mind during the test. When using the T-View Outline© make the extra effort to silently talk in your mind as you write down each idea so that you hear the words. When you are in a private place, experiment with talking to yourself out loud while writing down ideas. You may find that you learn information faster and more deeply than you do without sound.

- **Touch** – If this is your primary learning sense, you are probably athletic, or perhaps artistic. Regardless, you excel with your hands, and may even touch objects when a "DO NOT TOUCH" sign is displayed. You cannot help yourself. Your fingers are your information scanner, so taking notes is crucial for you. It will engage your mind and start to build a memory of what you are learning. When using the T-View Outline©, take the time to draw the T and write in the headings. Then write the ideas for both sides so that your mind can process all the information. Using the pencil or pen is a superb way to sharpen your memory and reduce the tendency for your thoughts to wander. You will find that you think better when you write than when you type. For you, key boards are not going to be the best way to absorb information, because it takes the feel out of your writing as well as the location on the paper where you are writing down your ideas. People, who touch, have the ability to remember where they wrote things on the page in their notes during a test and then recall it.

Even if you cannot figure out which sense is your primary learning sense, do not worry. You use them all anyway, and the magic of writing a T-View Outline© on paper is that it engages all three learning senses. This puts you at your best mentally, builds your confidence and generates a better list of ideas.

Benefits of Using the T-View Outline©

Now that we have a magic wand that creates time, increases the power of our thoughts and shows two sides of an issue, let's remind ourselves of the benefits of using the T-View Outline©:
- Seeing the highest scoring side of an issue
- Remembering all of our thoughts
- Producing a clean essay without scratched out words
- Writing a shorter essay
- Writing an essay that flows

Even if we stop right now and write our essay using the T-View Outline© as our guide, we are going to write a better essay. Building a T-View Outline© before we start writing is probably the most powerful action we can take to score a higher grade than normal.

There is more however. We can take a few moments to shape and harden our thinking, use techniques that simulate our teacher's two-view perspective and close the gap between their level of experience and ours.

Come along with us and read sections 1-B and 1-C as we make our essay bulletproof. For those who would rather just start writing, feel free to go forward to Phase 2 of our Game Plan, STAGE, page 75, but beware, your teacher may shoot your essay full of holes!

1-B. How to De-BUGS© the Ideas

Unseen Gaps

We now have two lists of ideas in ***Dogs vs. Cats***. We could write our essay from either one, but what if there is a bad idea in our list that our teacher will notice and deduct points for mentioning. How do we find it? We will dip into the world of technology and borrow a technique video game developers use to make sure that the software they write will run defect free.

Video game developers write their software in one task and then check it for errors in a second task. Developers view the task of creating software as separate from the task of making sure it is of high quality. The jargon for this second phase is "debugging" the software, a term that dates back to the early days of computers. Back then, the machines filled rooms, and memory chips were rows of vacuum tubes (think light bulbs). A bug (insect) once flew into the room of vacuum tubes, wedged itself into the connection between a tube and the computer and shorted out the connection. When the programmer removed the fried bug, she remarked that she had "debugged" the computer. The dramatic view of the fried bug launched the term into everyday use.

Like video game developers, we are going to view the creating of our ideas (T-View Outline©) as a different activity from making sure that our ideas are defect free. We will take the beloved debug term and build the acronym **De-BUGS©** from it. The letters **B U G S** stand for the four tests we will put our ideas through to assure their quality. Our tests will look for **B**reakdowns in logic, **U**niversal principles in play, **G**laring weaknesses and potential changes in the **S**ystem. Once we have checked our ideas for gaps in thought, we will write knowing that our ideas are sound and that we are immune to most "trick questions."

STRATEGY TOOL #3:   Create a rationally sound essay by looking for gaps in four areas:
- **B**reakdowns in logic
- **U**niversal principles in play
- **G**laring weaknesses
- **S**ystem changes

We will now go through our ideas for dogs on the left side of our T-View Outline© and look for **B U G S**.

Breakdowns in Logic

Finding lapses in our logic requires common sense. In this section, we look at how to get common sense even when we suspect that we do not have it. The joke about common sense has always been that *"it is not very common."* So then, how do we achieve this admired, simple, yet elusive skill? **We get common sense by asking the question:** *"How does this work?"*

As curious people, we keep asking questions. Once we can explain something to somebody else, draw it on the board or use it to solve a problem, we know that we have a basis for common sense about it. Now we still need to use our mind and refine that understanding. When facing a new situation, we apply our understanding to it and watch how it fits – always seeking a deeper grasp of the concept. We don't stop asking, *"How does this work?"*

If we stop searching too soon, we end up with partial knowledge of how something works and open ourselves up to a **B**reakdown in our essay's logic. I watch for breakdowns around me as I go through life, and here is one of the more memorable ones, where partial knowledge led to a **B**reakdown in logic.

Scene: Christmas vacation, my younger sister is on college break and she has a new boyfriend – as usual. The boyfriend is serving in the Coast Guard. His goal in life is to be captain of his own lobster boat. Meanwhile, the family dentist drops in and joins the celebration. Conversation turns to our brother, Forrest, who is living overseas in the Philippines.

Sister: Let's call Forrest and wish him a Merry Christmas!

Dentist: That would be great. Wow, how far away are the Philippines, anyway?

Boyfriend: About 13,000 miles.

Dentist: I wonder what day it is over there. Well, if it's Sunday here, thirteen thousand miles away, Hmmm… must be at least Tuesday over there!

Boyfriend: It's Monday…

Dentist: The Philippines are at least two days away.

Boyfriend: That's impossible, there's only <u>one</u> day at a time on the entire planet.

Dentist: *That's not true; there is Greenwich Mean Time in Europe, that starts each day. Then there is an international date line in the Pacific. Japan is always at least a day ahead, Europe is always a day behind, so you already have two days right there. With the Philippines even further than Japan, I'd say Forrest is at least two, maybe even three days ahead of us!*

Boyfriend: *Look, I'm in the Coast Guard, in navigation, and I'm telling you there aren't more than 24 hours around the globe, ever, anywhere.*

Dentist: *Look, I'm a Dentist and I'm telling you that Forrest is two days away from us here in Boston. If it's Sunday here, it's Tuesday there!*

Sister: *All right! All right! Let's call Forrest in the Philippines and ask him what day it is. He'll know.*

Sometimes we allow our emotions, in the passion of the moment, to disconnect our brain. Had the Dentist figured out how the solar system works, he would never have tried to argue his undefendable position. The 24-hours on the earth are labeled between 1 and 2 dates at any moment. Who would ever attempt to prove that one person on earth was two days (48 hours) ahead of another? Someone who had never put out the mental effort to figure out how days work from a planetary perspective. Someone who was not curious – that's who.

A curious person draws out the solar system on a piece of paper or plays with a flashlight and a basketball in a dark room until she figures out how the Sun creates a day on the Earth. When we learn how things work by playing with objects and drawing pictures, we never forget – because we were there when the understanding happened. The best way to cut down on studying is to play around with new ideas we learn in school until we understand how things work. Taking the time to play around with the things our teachers present and figuring out how things work eliminates hours of study later – because we <u>already</u> know.

The earth rotates around the sun and spins on its axis. One complete spin of the earth on its axis equals one day. One rotation of the earth around the sun equals one year. These are the two key movements and there is only one source of light. At any moment in time, roughly half the earth is in darkness while the other half faces the light of the sun. This means there is only one "day" and one "night" on the globe at a time. Typically, it takes 12 hours to spin through the darkness or the light. Human created time zones may label two different dates on the globe at the same time, but never more than 24-hours. Therefore, one spot is never more than one day ahead of another.

> **PERFORMANCE SECRET #3: Achieve common sense by being <u>curious</u> and asking *"How does this work?"***

Now, applying this secret to writing essays, we ask questions about each idea in the T-View Outline© individually and of all the ideas collectively. We are sniffing out **B**reakdowns in our logic. Here are some questions I ask myself when looking at our list for dogs that prove they deliver more value than cats:
- *How does this work?*
- *Does this make sense?*
- *Is this always true?*
- *Where is this not true?*
- *When is this not true?*
- *Am I being consistent?*

We now take a deeper look at these probing questions:

- **How work** – We addressed this above on the preceding page where we suggested drawing the situation out, using objects around the house such as flashlights to figure out physical phenomena, and most importantly we suggest here that the student asks questions of people they know, to find out what others know on a subject. Use all resources at your disposal.

- **Make Sense** – Does it make sense that dogs deliver more value? Well, dogs cost more than cats; money is a practical measure of value in society, we can walk into a pet store and compare price tags between cats and dogs. The average cat with shots costs $60 while the average dog costs $400. So yes, it makes sense that dogs are more valuable.

- **Idea True** – Is this true? Work is the primary way humans generate value in their societies. When we add unpaid efforts such as homemaking and volunteering as real work, we can reach nearly 100% of people in society generating value. Well, there are more working dogs than working cats. We are not aware of any cats going to work with their masters. Dogs go to work with humans in many areas. We see Dalmatians riding on fire trucks, St. Bernards rescue-ready at ski resorts and German Shepherds on patrol with Police. Given this, we have seen with our own eyes that the value dogs deliver to society daily is greater than cats based on participation level. Therefore, yes, the idea is true that dogs generate more value than cats.

- **Where or When is this not true** – The power of this question is that we only need to find one exception to a good idea to realize it is a bad idea – if the exception is strong enough. We now look deeper at how we define working cats. What if a farmer considers his cat to be working on the farm by reducing the mice and rat populations? How much value is that cat generating? In the early half of the last century in the United States, family farms produced significant amounts of foodstuffs. Given the extent to which family farms have dwindled in the past sixty years very few cats work on farms today. Although we have identified a situation where our idea is not true, we have figured out that the frequency of this is so rare today; there is no defect in our pro-dog position.

- **Being Consistent** – A fundamental way to avoid a **B**reakdown in logic is to be consistent. For example, if we plan to prove that cats deliver more value to society, we might build up the angle of cats being great indoor pets. Part of that build up will inevitably be the need to de-claw their paws. Later in the essay, we may choose to present the idea that cats are vital to public health because their predatory instincts keep rodent populations in check. Rats, mice and other rodents are unsanitary. Here is the problem with advancing both of these ideas in the same essay. Cats require their claws to stop rats. Cats must be declawed to be non-destructive indoor pets. It is inconsistent and impossible for a cat to both have and not have its claws at the same time. Therefore, we must leave the weaker idea out or explain that different cats deliver different benefits. If we ignore the inconsistency, the grader will assume a **B**reakdown in our logic, write those dreaded critical comments in red ink on our paper and lower our grade accordingly. Being consistent is a key way to avoid a **B**reakdown in logic.

Universal Principles in Play

Universal principles are the most likely place to find tricks in an essay question. We usually fall prey to a trick question by getting distracted in the details, and we forget about an overriding principle, a force or a key concept introduced earlier in the course. In that moment, we have lost perspective on how important one principle is relative to another. Math provides us with a simple illustration of how this happens. If we multiply several positive and negative numbers together, we may come up with the right digits in our answer. However, if we forget to account for just one of the minus signs, the polarity in our answer is off and we are 100% wrong. Even though -43 and 43 look similar, they are mathematically different by a value of 86, twice either's absolute value. There is a principle that says a number's polarity (being either positive or negative) defines the value of the number, not just the number itself. On essay questions, principles and laws affect our arguments as strongly as polarity affects math. Here are some everyday examples in school and life where Universal principles are in play with overriding force:

- **Physics** – Whenever we are working with a physics problem, Universal principles (usually defined as forces) are in play. Gravity is a prime example. Regardless of how well we figure out the arithmetic that involves mass and acceleration, if we forget about gravity we will come up with the wrong answer, having forgotten about friction, the byproduct of gravity. If we are vigilantly looking for these Universal principles, we will prevail on physics exams.

- **Shopping** – The price we pay for goods and services is a result of how badly other people want what we want. The store is going to sell the blue jeans we have our heart set on for a price that allows them to find buyers for every single pair of jeans. If we really want the jeans, we are going to have to get there early and pay full price. If we wait for a sale, we may find that the jeans in our size are out of stock when we get to the store. On the other hand, if the jeans are not as desirable to others as to us, we can wait until the store lowers the price to an amount we want to pay. The Universal principle we are talking about is Supply and Demand. Want is Demand. Supply is the inventory of jeans in the store. As shoppers, we will buy the jeans we want at the price that matches our value for the jeans. As sellers, we will lower our price until we sell all of our jeans. This principle of Supply and Demand is Universal because it is in play every time people buy and sell products and services.

- **Fast Cars** – Many people like to drive fast. If you doubt this, consider how many people driving today in America exceed the speed limit. A short drive on any freeway would lead anyone to the conclusion that most drivers exceed the speed limit. Since many drivers enjoy driving fast, they often seek to buy faster cars. Drivers rely on numbers to tell them which cars to buy; especially the horsepower of the engine, because more horsepower means more speed, right?

Which Car is Faster?

Red 2008 sports car powered by 505 horsepower engine

Red 2008 muscle car powered by 540 horsepower engine

The correct answer is that it depends. What does it depend on? All the numbers that define the **U**niversal Principle – Speed. If we took the information the "test" question gave us on the previous page, we would choose the muscle car as the faster car because it had 35 more horsepower; 540 to 505. When we actually drive the cars, we find out that the made-in-America sports car with 505 horsepower accelerates to 60 miles per hour in 3.7 seconds, while the wildly popular muscle car accelerates to 60 miles per hour in 4.7 seconds. How can the car with less horsepower go faster? What is missing here? We do not understand how the **U**niversal Principle of Speed works!

The sports car is one second faster, which in the world of automobile performance is light years. How can this happen? Is this a trick question? No. Nothing is wrong here other than the thought process that *"more horsepower always means more speed."* This belief ignores physics. The **U**niversal physics principle that explains speed is acceleration equals force divided by mass, or **a=f/m**. This is simply another view of **f=ma** (force equals mass times acceleration).

This means that a lighter car (smaller mass) with a less powerful engine (force) could outperform a heavier car (larger mass) with a more powerful engine (force) depending upon which fraction is bigger. Students who know that speed comes from a mathematical equation, a **U**niversal physics principle, are looking for two numbers when asked which car is faster: horsepower (**f**) and weight (**m**). The sports car weighs 3,190 pounds and the muscle car weighs 3,885 pounds. Now we know enough to answer the question. Notice that the sports car weighs 695 pounds less and this difference is much bigger in a fraction than the difference of 35 horsepower.

A car nut will tell you that other factors go into this equation: suspension, tires, road conditions and the driver's skills – to name a few. However, our example above assumes that all other things remain constant, which is how most test questions in a physics class are set up.

There are some students who would believe that the question, ***"Which car is faster?"*** was a trick question. However, the open-minded reader will perceive that trick questions come from lack of knowledge. The question is only deceptive to those who did not **THINK** to find the **U**niversal Principle relating to speed, **f=ma**.

Students who focus on what **U**niversal principles are in play, know the information to look out for, and not only end up "studying" less – they get more test questions right!

Finding the Boundaries

Another secret to avoiding trick questions is to find out what the boundaries are for that course or test and to identify the **U**niversal principles that operate within those boundaries. Some **U**niversal principles only exist in a limited scope. Electricity is something that works in a **U**niversal way within boundaries. As long as the element through which we are attempting to observe electric current is a conductor, the behaviors of electricity will apply and be predictable. Electricity also demonstrates the need for boundaries, for without a conductor the electricity cannot be transported with predictability. At times, we may be writing an essay on a subject with apparently no boundaries. For example, when studying a discipline such as theology, the boundaries can become by definition – infinite. When discussing the Creator, God or Heavenly Father, we are considering a **U**niversal Being who existed before anything we can define as a boundary. He is a clear example of someone beyond boundaries.

From time to time, we approach a boundary with similar infinite characteristics in science, when we find that the behavior of sub-atomic particles is orderly and consistent and approaching the limits of what we can observe. We also work with the concept of infinity when playing in the wonderful discipline of mathematics. We start with the discovery of the irrational number π (pi) and advance in Calculus with taking things to the limit without ever reaching them.

Mostly on tests, we are operating within <u>tightly</u> <u>defined</u> boundaries. When we get confused while answering an essay question, it is usually because we are not clear about what the boundaries are and therefore cannot tell which **U**niversal principles are in play. Finding the courage to ask our teacher "dumb" questions in class, like these below, pays off huge on test day:

- *Why do you [my teacher] **repeatedly emphasize** _____?*
- *Which laws exist here?*
- *What do these laws make available to happen?*

Then on test day:
- *What tone of voice does my teacher use to tell us what is most important? What did he say in that tone?*
- *In what way does this idea on my T-View Outline© forget a **U**niversal principle?*
- *Which laws are in play?*

- **Teacher Emphasis** – This is probably the biggest clue of them all. When our teacher repeats topics, principles, or concepts; the repetition is a sign that she is reemphasizing a **U**niversal principle or its effects. Once identified, it is vital to understand all the different ways a **U**niversal principle works in the subject of study. While repetitive conversations on the same phenomenon are a red flag warning that the teacher is talking about a **U**niversal principle, our personal curiosity and persistence will ensure that we know which **U**niversal principles in play and give us the working knowledge to identify them in all their varied disguises.

- **Laws in Play** – During a physics test, I once became stuck attempting to find all the numbers I needed to solve a problem. The question provided a reactionary force. What I needed was the causative force – but the question did not provide it. I was quite distraught, thinking that the teacher had made a mistake. Then I remembered Newton's Third Law of motion. It was in play, because it is <u>always</u> in play! *"For every action there is an equal and opposite reaction."* I found my missing piece by taking the opposite value of the number I was given. Seemingly, out of nowhere, I had magically created the missing information. I could trust my thought process because I knew, as a **U**niversal principle; Newton's Third Law is <u>always</u> in play. This story highlights why it is important for us to be aware of all the laws in play, even if they *"aren't on the test."*

- **Law Makes Available** – Every law gives us a specific "box" of knowing. As mentioned earlier, in physics, force equals mass times acceleration, **f=ma**. This always gives us three numbers even if the question only provides two. This is because we can get the other value by crunching a mathematical equation. Supply and Demand in our shopping example, always gives us many different prices at which blue jeans are bought and sold. Sometimes, the essay question provides all the information required to answer it when we remember the **U**niversal principle in play. Often times the answer key to the essay is simply explaining how the **U**niversal principle applies to the question.

- **Forget Principle** – We can always look at our list of ideas on the **T-View Outline**© and check each one for where it will not work – because a **U**niversal principle is in play!

Universal principles are the measuring stick we use to test our ideas in the T-View Outline©. Taking the time to think these through is a valuable use of our time. It is better to think through our point of view now and change it while it is one word, than to write many sentences in an essay, only to find out that our ideas are not sound. In essay writing, quality always wins out over quantity.

PERFORMANCE SECRET #4: Avoid trick questions by identifying the **U**niversal principles and the boundaries they operate within.

Glaring Weaknesses

Sometimes we present an idea, thinking it is a great reason for our thesis to be true – when in reality it is ammunition for the other side. Consider also traveling in a moving vehicle, in which the driver is blinded by the glare from the sun. The problem is that you are still moving forward. Both ammunition for the other side and a blind driver are dangerous – one to your grade and the other to your health. The best way to uncover a blind spot in an idea is to THINK by asking these questions:

- ***Who does this idea benefit the most? Us or Them?***
- ***If it benefits them, how can I make it benefit me?***

For example, as I considered my list of ideas for dogs, I realized two ideas about dogs made the cats look better. The strong ideas were on the wrong side of the **T-View Outline**©. Allow me to explain:

- **Benefit Us or Them?** – Cats are easy to feed while the owner is on vacation especially with the deployment of automatic feeding devices. Dogs cannot compete with this, since they require regular feeding of larger quantities and variety. The clean-up at the other end makes this more apparent. While a cat owner can use an indoor litter box, dogs require a kennel, large yard or walk with poop scoop technology. This vast difference in care weighs heavily in favor of cats. On first glance, we should leave this idea out of our essay. However, on second glance we might be able to convert this into a positive. This brings us to the popular word: Spin.

- **How can I make it benefit me?** – Now that we have identified feeding and walking as a **G**laring weakness for dogs delivering the most value, we seek to make it benefit dogs with some Spin. Some Spin strategies are:

    1 – **Search for Facts** such as medical studies showing that people who owned dogs lived longer. Perhaps the daily action of walking the dog lowered their stress levels. The idea is *"America's healthcare issues would go down if more people were out walking their dogs, an activity that reduces human stress while providing the dog with exercise and an opportunity to relieve itself outside the owner's home."*

    2 – **Rely on ideas based upon common perceptions** such as that owners often treat their dogs as people. *"The time a dog owner spends feeding and walking his dog creates a bond of love between the owner and the dog. This love lowers the owner's physical stress and blood pressure, which leads to a healthier mental and emotional life. These benefits are not possible with the non-walkable cat."*

3 – Take a human benefit and attach it to the dog:
"Physicians often encourage their patients to take brisk 20 minute walks three to five times per week because walking increases health. However, people seldom demonstrate the self-discipline to exercise daily. What better reminder exists than a dog who will nudge you with her nose and yelp until you take her outside on a daily basis?"

After thinking through how convincing the Spin on our three options are, we decide that they are all pretty weak given the alternatives to exercise motivation. Taking care of a dog is much more work than that for a cat and the odds are that the teacher will figure this out. Therefore, we simply draw a line through these weak ideas – and move on.

DOGS BEST	CATS BEST
– WORK	– SOFT ☺
– SIGHT DOGS	– KILL RATS
– POLICE K-9	– SELF CLEANING
– BITE THIEVES	– BABY SIT SELF
– RACING	– ~~BUY FOR FREE~~
– PLAY CATCH	– ~~HAVE~~
– PROTECT FAMILY	– ~~PLAY~~
– ~~LIVE 10-14 YEARS~~	– 12-16 YEAR LIFE
– HANG OUT	
– ~~WALK 2X A DAY~~	– MOST POPULAR
– TRAINABLE	– ~~LESS~~
– BARK LOUD	

Strike out clear benefit for the other side

*Strike out **G**laring Weakness*

It is wise to leave out any ideas that assist the other side or require too much spin. Thanks to the T-View Outline©, dumping bad ideas early is simple. In the old way of writing essays, we may have written a few pages before we realized that we had a bad idea. There may not be time to recover from this. By thinking first, our bad ideas are gone before we even start writing – resulting in a more convincing and higher scoring essay.

> **PERFORMANCE SECRET #5:** Identify <u>G</u>laring weaknesses by asking: *"Who does this idea benefit the most? Us or Them?"*

Potential System Changes

Now we will discuss the "**S**" in the **De-BUGS**© strategy where **S** stands for System. Many of us know someone (perhaps it is even ourselves) who is fascinated by the mysterious disappearance of Dinosaurs 65 Million years ago. While most of us can agree that Dinosaurs are either exciting or over-hyped, the scientific community cannot agree on exactly how they became extinct. One thing is clear about their extinction – there was a radical change in the Dinosaurs' environment that caused them to die out.

Something happened to the ecological "**S**ystem" in which they lived and the Dinosaurs could not handle the change. Some scientists believe the event that altered the Dinosaurs' **S**ystem was an incoming asteroid hitting the planet with such size and power that the ecosystem supporting the Dinosaurs became unavailable for an extended period. Without sunlight plants died and without plants Dinosaurs died of starvation. Other scientists believe it was a steep drop in sea levels, while still others insist massive volcanic eruptions destroyed their environment. Geology does record radical climate changes; on that much we can agree. Patterns in rock created millions of years ago show that the biological **S**ystem in which Dinosaurs lived altered fundamentally in a very short timeframe. Any one of the possible causes for the Dinosaurs' extinction is an example of a "potential **S**ystem change." For the Dinosaurs, it was not potential. It was reality. In the world of essays, we are often writing about potential – what could have happened or could happen. Observing how a <u>potential</u> change can affect the normal **S**ystem in which our essay resides generates deep insight and unique ideas. Developing original insight and ideas is the ticket to higher grades.

With a little imagination, we can mentally adapt anything we are writing about into a **S**ystem. For example, a chemistry experiment, a computer **S**ystem, the process of photosynthesis in a plant, the nation's economic **S**ystem, an assembly line at General Motors, a ballet, or the group of friends we hang out with are all **S**ystems. We <u>define</u> the **S**ystem by <u>what</u> we <u>put</u> <u>in</u> it. This is where we start owning the gap between the teacher and the test. We start to experiment by imagining the system in our mind, making changes to the system and observing the result. Now we start to create ideas our teachers will reward.

We take that **S**ystem we just invented in our own mind, and watch how all the parts interact with each other. What are the relationships and connections between the components? **S**ystems are in motion, which means there are causes and effects. Forces are generated in our **S**ystem. We can start to see factors that make the **S**ystem work. We see what happens when the **S**ystem goes in different directions. When writing an essay, it is highly beneficial to figure out <u>what</u> <u>changes</u> in the **S**ystem <u>are</u> <u>possible</u>, <u>not</u> <u>possible</u>, <u>likely</u> or <u>not likely</u>.

We look for clues to potential **S**ystem changes by identifying what is already there in the **S**ystem that can make it unstable. For example, if an asteroid did hit the earth and destroyed the environment, had the Dinosaurs looked into telescopes and possessed the intelligence to use them, they would have seen the asteroid *already there* in space and realized that its path was on a trajectory to hit the earth. Bringing the *already there* concept to the present day, let's say we park our expensive sports car with chrome wheels on the street in the south side of Chicago and leave town for a week. The thieves, who steal every part off the car, leaving a rusty frame and dangling electrical wires, were *already there* in the social **S**ystem of the neighborhood before we parked. In fact, the cinderblocks the car is now resting upon were *already* lying around before the car arrived. An outcome like this is no mystery to the enlightened sports car owner, if he sees who and what is *already there* in the **S**ystem of the inner-city neighborhood.

PERFORMANCE SECRET #6: Find deep insights by identifying the potential changes *already there* in the System.

Here are the questions I like to ask myself as I review each idea on my T-View Outline© while looking for potential changes in the **S**ystem:
- *What is possible in my system?*
- *What forces already exist that could affect my system?*
- *Is there anything out there that could wipe out my system?*
- *How likely is this?*
- *How believable is this?*

Back to the **T-View Outline**© for ***Dogs vs. Cats***, as I consider each idea under dogs, I depend on the strength of my thesis, the fact that dogs have the skill to follow verbal commands. Within this strength, I look at:

- **What is possible** – Anyone who has been to privileged to watch live performances of Dolphins and Killer Whales knows how consistently the mammals follow signals and commands. Trainability is possible. Yet, specific to our question, is it possible to achieve a similar breakthrough with cats? There are no current scientific research projects *already there* working to achieve a breakthrough in cat communication. Therefore, we can conclude that nothing already exists in the "**S**ystem" to counter a dog's unique superiority to follow spoken commands. In truth, nothing has been there during the last four thousand years of human/cat communication (the **S**ystem) to give the cat advocates any hope.

- **Other Forces** – In California, the next earthquake lurks below ground, specifically along the San Andreas Fault. Earthquakes are not only possible but also likely along this jagged line. Therefore, a potential force *already there* regarding the value a Police Dog in California is earthquakes. Earthquakes could disorientate dogs as well as people. We consider that War Dogs operate in a similar chaotic environment, one of exploding bombs, crackling fires, falling buildings, speeding battle tanks, thundering helicopters and sporadic gunshots. None of these situations affects the War Dogs' ability to obey spoken commands and perform as trained; hence, we can transfer this success to our California earthquake scenario and conclude that earthquakes will not interfere with dogs' ability to perform Police K-9 duties.

- **Anything Wipe Out** – Is there anything possible, or in the **S**ystem that could remove all dogs from planet earth? For example, a rare disease affecting only dogs' DNA could appear and wipe out the entire species. This is not far-fetched. A similar situation *already* exists in the world with another species. The Tasmanian devil, living in Australia, is threatened at the time of this writing by the devil facial tumor disease. Their mean behavior is a force in their social **S**ystem that can easily wipe out this population. The fatal disease is transferred during the normal social behavior of the Tasmanian Devil – fighting. This creates a physical dilemma to nature preservationists. Tasmanian Devils must be separated from each other to prevent the fighting, but the devils must be put together to mate. Without mating, the species will die out in one generation. These two mutually exclusive requirements for the species' survival threaten it to extinction. Returning to our essay, we are not aware of any diseases *already there* among dogs that threaten their extinction. Therefore, we can conclude that nothing exists on the horizon that will wipe out dogs entirely as happened to the Dinosaurs.

- **Likelihood** – Now that we have looked at *What is Possible*, *Other Forces*, and *Anything Wipe Out*, another factor to consider is the perspective of our grader. Teachers consider how sound our argument is. Most of the time, the yardstick against which soundness is measured is reality; what is really going on out there in the world. Likelihood looks at the statistical probability of something happening. The likelihood of a woman giving birth to a boy is 49% and a girl is 51%. It is very likely that a pregnant woman will have a child – close to 100%. Building a case that all pregnant women will give birth to girls is unlikely, and makes for a thesis out of touch with reality. It is important to leave out unlikely potential **S**ystem changes since we will lose credibility with the grader when presenting them.

- **Believability** – How believable is this potential change in the **S**ystem? Believability is different from Likelihood. While likelihood is a statistical measurement, believability is an emotional measurement. An earthquake in southern California is believable because the region already experiences earthquakes frequently. However, is it believable that dogs can be counted on to follow spoken commands during a natural disaster such as earthquakes?

  As mentioned above, we can draw on something *already there* (War Dogs) in the **S**ystem of our essay (Real Life), and present the illustration that War Dogs such as German Shepherds follow spoken commands in earthquake like conditions. This example illustrates why it is important to give our teachers the reasons behind our ideas. Visit pages 127-131 to learn how to write reasons into your essay. Ideas become believable when we present evidence to support them.

  Many graders focus on the believable outcomes. It is wise to size up our teacher and observe whether he makes decisions based upon facts or emotions. Then we can assess Likelihood and Believability for a specific grader. Regardless of our teacher's personality, it is our job as students to bring to light facts, examples and information that support our ideas. The T-View Outline© is the perfect place to look and THINK to generate this evidence.

Conclusion on **BUGS**

We have just absorbed four dialogues on what it means to THINK. Each idea on our **T-View Outline©** was reviewed for **B**reakdowns in logic, **U**niversal principles in play, **G**laring weaknesses and potential **S**ystem changes. Having put our ideas through these four rigorous tests, we can now write about them with the confidence that they are sound.

1-C. Defuse the Counter-Ideas

Being Proactive

We will now explain the "De" in front of our **BUGS** tool and make it a complete **De-BUGS**© tool. In our **De-BUGS**© acronym, De stands for the word "Defuse." Our analogy considers terrorism. If a terrorist plants a bomb in a public place, the bomb squad goes in and takes apart the bomb's ability to explode – thereby making the explosive useless. We define this action as "defusing" the bomb.

The parallel we draw between the real world explosive and the ideas in our essay is that we could present an idea that would be dangerous to our thesis. It is also possible that someone proving an opposite point of view (cats) could present an idea that would unravel our dogs thesis. Regardless of the source of unraveling, if we can neutralize the counter idea that hurts our thesis – we defuse and eliminate the threat. This is an extremely valuable skill in the theoretical realm of school. Therefore, we will now reveal ways to <u>defuse threats</u> to our <u>thesis</u> by leveraging the information in our T-View Outline©.

Defuse the Dangerous Counter-Idea

We defuse a counter-idea by thinking about it twice. First we THINK about their strongest idea and how that is a negative for us. Second, we THINK about where their strongest idea is weak. The value of the second THINK is that we can then use their weakness to discredit their position. Even if we do a poor job of discrediting their strength, we neutralize the strength simply by bringing it up. It is now nearly impossible for the teacher to lay down red ink and deduct grade points by pointing out that we missed their "stunning insight."

It is smart to mention strengths of the opposing point of view before our grader does. The truth is that our grader already knows about it anyway. She has far more experience with this question and the course subject than we do. By the time the grader gets to our written response, she most likely will have read hundreds or even thousands of responses to this same question or one very similar to it. The notion that we can simply ignore threatening counter-ideas in the hope that the grader might miss them is pure fantasy. Our primary goal here is to write a convincing essay, and when we mention the pros and cons of our point-of-view, we deny the grader the justification she needs to subtract points for presenting an incomplete analysis. The strategies in this defuse section minimize the effect of mentioning the opposing strength.

A sound essay considers the strengths and weaknesses of both sides and makes a convincing argument for one side. Along the way, the essay shows how we balance the trade-offs of strengths and weaknesses in our own mind. The popular approach of ignoring opposing strengths keeps the grader in the dark about our thought process. We appear to either lack knowledge of the material or the presence of mind to discuss the pros and cons. Neither of these impressions will improve our grade.

The **First THINK** - As we survey the cat side on the right in the T-View Outline©, we look for ways to prove that cats deliver more value. Typical questions to ask are:
- *Which strength carries the day?*
- *What is the strength of cats as a whole package?*
- *Why would someone believe cats deliver more value?*
- *As a Pro-dog person, where am I afraid to look?*

By answering these questions, we find a number of ways that cats could make a more convincing essay than the one we are planning for dogs. In our stack of cat ideas, we have identified three dangerous counter-ideas:
- **Kill rats**
- **Buy for free**
- **Most popular**

DOGS BEST	CATS BEST
— WORK	— SOFT :")
— SIGHT DOGS	— **(KILL RATS)**
— POLICE K-9	— SELF CLEANING
— BITE THIEVES	— BABY SIT SELF
Dangerous counter ideas →	— **(BUY FOR FREE)**
— PLAY CATCH	— HAVE A LOT
— PROTECT FAMILY	— PLAYFUL
— ~~LIVE 10-14 YEARS~~	— 12-16 YEAR LIFE
— HANG OUT	
— ~~WALK 2x A DAY~~	— **(MOST POPULAR)**
— TRAINABLE	— LESS SHEDDING
— BARK LOUD	

The **Second THINK** – Now we look for the weakness in these cat strengths. We ask questions such as:
- *Where is the weakness in this idea?*
- *How is this strength not getting the job done?*
- *What is an easier way to provide this benefit?*
- *What do dogs have that is better than this?*

PERFORMANCE SECRET #7: Use the First THINK /Second THINK approach to find the defuse to a dangerous counter-idea.

Once we identify the counter-idea we want to defuse, there are two smart ways to do it. The first is the **Direct Approach**©. Here we attack the opposite point of view head-on and seize the initiative. The second is the **Replacement Approach**©. Here, we distract the reader's focus by presenting a better idea.

The Direct Approach©

When we seize the initiative, we control the timing of our graders' critical thought. Before he can think up a hole in our argument, we skillfully remove the hole. We do this by thinking up a counter-idea before he does. If successful, the grader is reacting to our counter-idea and we have the initiative. The benefit to us is that the grader will give us credit for thinking at a deeper level, which is the reason we were asked to respond to an essay question in the first place. We use any one of three tools to execute The Direct Approach©: **(1) Because**, **(2) Stating Evidence** or **(3) Comparison**.

(1) Because – *Because* is an easy word to use when connecting the cat strength with the reason it is not strong. For example, we could write,

> "Dogs are often trained to perform tasks. This daily training process takes time, repetition and maintenance. In the process, the human trainer bonds with the dog on a deep emotional level as he feeds, grooms and exercises the animal. This becomes a bonding experience rather than maintenance chores. Even though on first glance, it would appear that a cat's low maintenance would deliver higher value to society, this perceived low maintenance feature of cats loses its value when cats cannot provide the two-way bonding experience dogs do **because** cats cannot be trained to follow human spoken commands. Without this two-way communication, there is no deep bonding."

Notice that we do not have to spend significant time or detail on the cat's strength (low maintenance), we simply build the value of our counter-idea, and then mention a reason *because* to complete the defusing of the cat strength. Here is the psychology behind what we just did:

(a) **Acknowledge the negative**
"*Dogs are often trained to perform tasks. This daily training process takes time, repetition, and maintenance.*"

(b) **Minimize the effect**
"*In the process, the human trainer bonds with the dog on a deep emotional level as he feeds, grooms and exercises the animal. This becomes a bonding experience rather than maintenance chores.*"

(c) **Defuse the counter-idea's strength**
"*Even though on first glance, it would appear that a cat's low maintenance would deliver higher value to society, this*

*perceived low maintenance feature of cats loses its value when cats cannot provide the two-way bonding experience dogs do **because** cats cannot be trained to follow human spoken commands. Without this two way communication, there is no deep bonding."*

Notice that we must link the failure of the cat's companionship level to the cat's desirable maintenance factor. This devalues the cat's low maintenance strength by <u>association</u> rather than <u>proof</u>. If the pet is not delivering value, who cares how low its maintenance is? Even pet rocks deliver low maintenance. Notice that our defuse presents the dogs' weakness, minimizes it and defuses it all in one sentence (c). Here we accept the peril of writing a run-on sentence, since we must <u>link</u> <u>all</u> three <u>aspects</u> at the <u>same</u> <u>time</u> to <u>defuse</u> the cat's strength <u>effectively</u>.

Because is not the only word we can use to master this defuse. Other words include:
- since
- as a result of
- due to
- owing to

(2) State Evidence – We often hear people say *"Just the facts ma'am"* or joke *"Just the Fax"* but what truth does this joke really point to? Intuitively, we all seem to know that the best way to convince anyone of anything is to line up our facts. Facts in the classroom become key evidence on test day. Most textbooks even assist us by highlighting key facts in bold letters. How does this strategy compare to the **Because** approach? While the **Because** tool works by weighing perceived values, the **State Evidence** tool works by delivering an avalanche of proof. This is a quantity over precision approach. This is one place in The No-Study Solution© where we deviate somewhat from our rule that quality trumps quantity. Looking to our T-View Outline©, we choose the first idea, <u>work</u>; since there are many roles working dogs perform that we can pile up into a list of evidence.

DOGS BEST	CATS BEST
–WORK	– SOFT ☺
– SIGHT DOGS	– KILL RATS

(a) State Evidence

"Dogs deliver immense social value as evidenced by their participation in the workplace and recreational activities. Consider how many dogs perform police work, serve in the military, execute anti-terrorist patrols, find hidden drugs, guide the blind, tend flocks, protect homes and businesses, race on dog tracks, work at the fire station and play catch the flying disc in back yards, beaches and parks across America."

(b) Defuse the counter-idea's strength

"Given the numerous ways I have just mentioned that dogs serve humanity, it becomes obvious that the total value dogs deliver far exceeds the value of cats being popular."

We just named eleven pieces of evidence demonstrating dogs' value to counter one piece of evidence for cats. Many students would simply line up their eleven facts and believe they had won the argument. However, until we tell them **(b)** that we linked our dog strength to their cat strength and proved it with an avalanche of facts; we have not completed the job. There is no guarantee our grader will make the connection. It is <u>always</u> <u>vital</u> to <u>make</u> the <u>logical</u> <u>connections</u> <u>for</u> <u>her</u>. Also, consider how economical this three-sentence defuse is, the other option being to write a long logical case against the popularity of cats. Popularity in a democratic society can be quite persuasive.

(3) Comparison – Next we look at a pure comparison approach. We use this when the relative strengths of both ideas are close and we seek an edge. <u>Our</u> <u>intention</u> is to <u>make</u> the <u>perceived</u> <u>difference</u> <u>larger</u>. The psychology behind a comparison is to bring forward an idea that is emotionally charged or dramatic enough to achieve a higher perceived value in the reader's mind.

Suppose our concern is that Americans own more pet cats than pet dogs. At the time of this writing, cats are more popular by 16 million. This number is a fact. How could 16 million choices be wrong? We have circled this idea in the T-View Outline© on the following page. Rather than take this fact on directly, we will compare it to something more emotionally powerful than popularity – life itself. We will use the dual-word-pair ***Not only /but also!***

Not only/but also –

*"Dogs **not only** save people's lives on a frequent basis, as reported in the news on Web and TV, **but also** achieve this while cats outnumber them by 16 million. Imagine how many more lives would be saved if the 16 million cat owners traded in their Fluffy for Fido?"*

DOGS BEST	CATS BEST
– WORK	– SOFT :)
– SIGHT DOGS	– KILL RATS
– POLICE K-9	– SELF CLEANING
– BITE THIEVES	– BABY SIT SELF
– RACING	– BUY FOR FREE
– PLAY CATCH	– HAVE A LOT
– PROTECT FAMILY	– PLAYFUL
– ~~LIVE 10-14 YEARS~~	– 12-16 YEAR LIFE
– ~~HANG OUT~~	
– ~~A DAY~~	– **MOST POPULAR**
– ~~LE~~	– LESS SHEDDING
– BARK LOUD	

The Cat's dangerous counter idea → MOST POPULAR

Additionally/yet – Another effective word pair:

"**Additionally**, cats are not known to save people in danger, **yet** a dog saved four kittens by standing guard and leading the firefighters to their bed in a burning Australian home in October of 2008. This selfless act by a dog demonstrates that it is always ready to deliver value, trained or untrained; the dog instinctively knows how to save people and other animals in danger. This example underscores how broad a dog's value to society is, spanning both loyalty and courage."

The emotional hook influences our grader beyond pure logic. We are comparing the lack of cats' protective skills with their popularity. Even though these are incongruent, the logical grader will think, "*Where was the mother cat?*"

STRATEGY TOOL #4: Defuse with The Direct Approach© by using a *Because, State Evidence* or *Comparison*.

The Replacement Approach©

When the Direct Approach© does not seem to fit, we use a deflection strategy which means we present a more attractive option to the reader. We call this deflection, the Replacement Approach© because we are going to replace their good idea with our better idea. The value of this approach is that the two ideas do not have to match.

For example, we can clearly see that cats, being predators, hunt down rats, mice and other filthy rodents, killing them. Rats operate at night and avoid humans. This requires a non-human solution to destroy them. Rats live in unsanitary conditions and consequently spread disease. Fewer rodents mean a healthier neighborhood. A "Cats Best" essay argues that cats provide greater health to all homes in the neighborhood, including those homes with dogs and no cats. Therefore, cats provide more value overall to society. Those of us writing a "Dogs Best" essay spot this counter-idea and quickly circle it on the T-View Outline©.

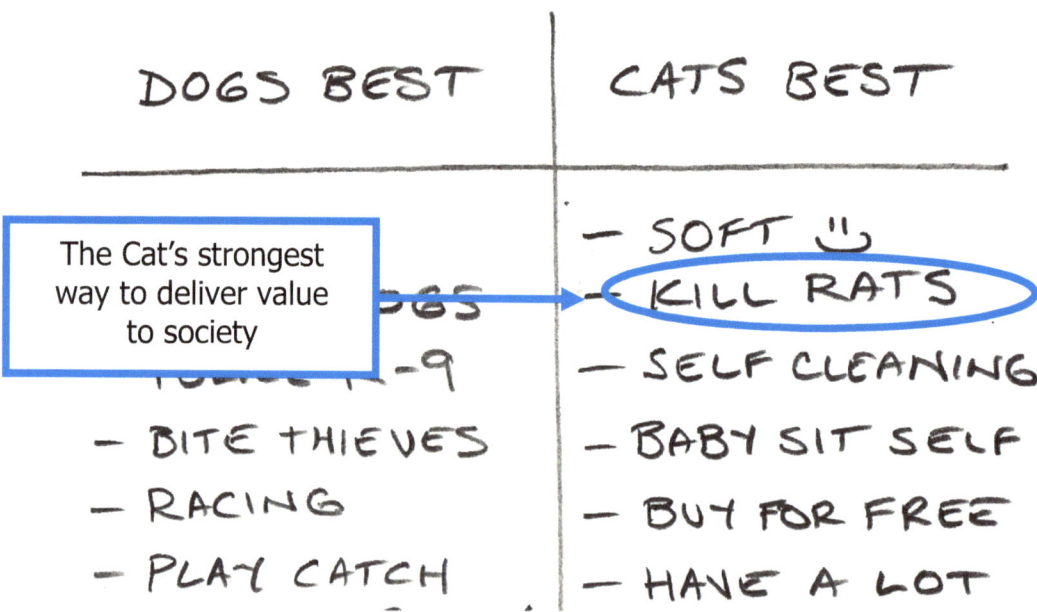

Now, we reach back to our **Second THINK** questions on page 63, and ask, *"Is there an easier way to provide this benefit?"* We ponder it and realize the answer is... yes! People today already use low cost and readily available rat poison. They place it around the homestead to eliminate rats. Consider how convenient and cheap it is to purchase rat poison, tear open the cardboard box and set it out, compared to caring for a cat over its 15-year life span. As of this writing, a 16-piece box of a popular brand of rat poison sells for $18.67 on Amazon.com. Cats incur ongoing costs that start in the hundreds of dollars for immunizations as kittens, and rise to the thousands for veterinarian bills as they age. Add to that, the ongoing weekly food and shelter costs, and $18.67 is a persuasive argument.

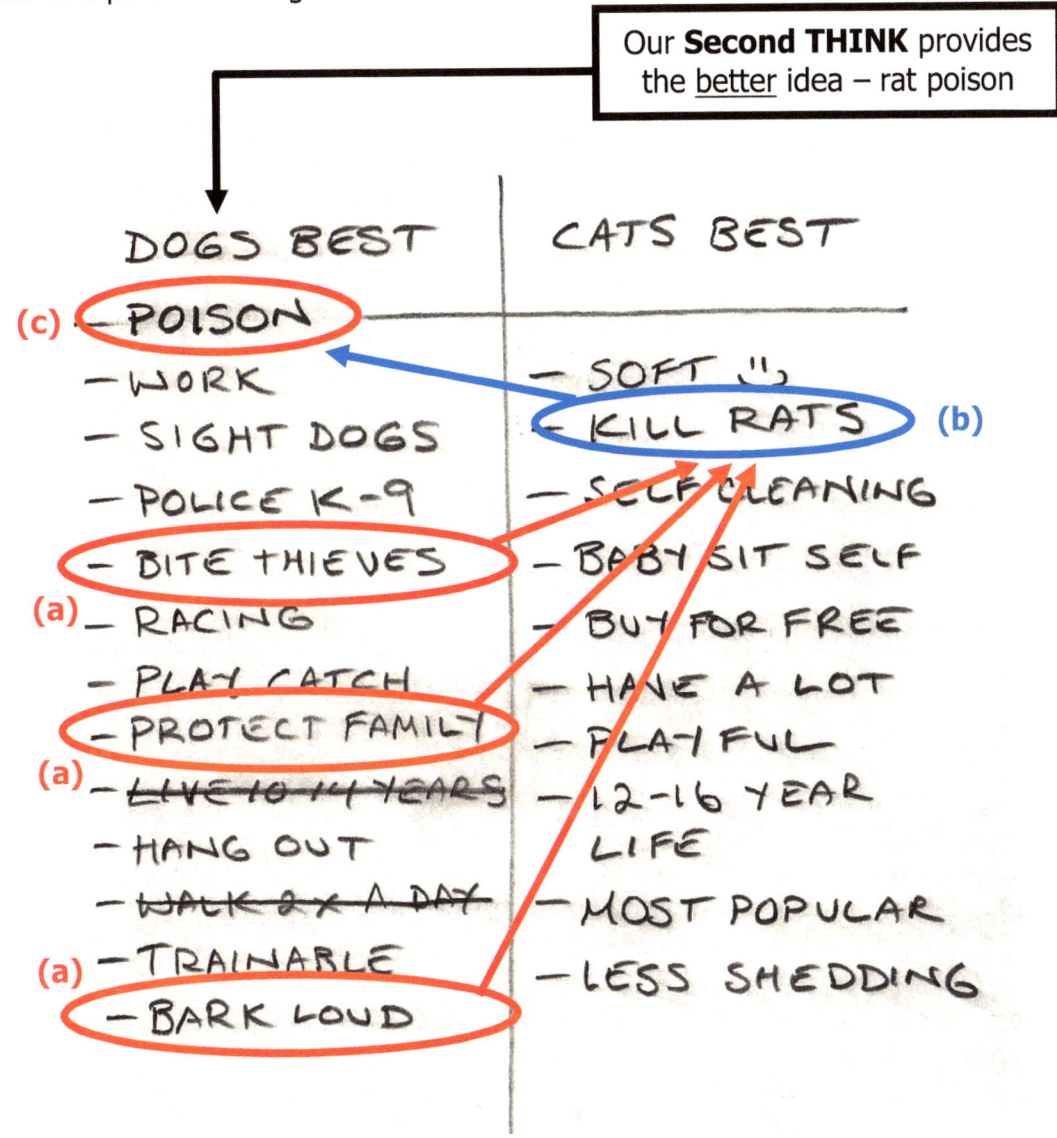

Now we will execute a defuse of this cat strength by <u>replacing</u> it with a completely logical and viable alternative: rat poison, as illustrated by going from **(a)** to **(b)** to **(c)**, as follows:

(a) Strong dog idea
Dogs contribute to public safety across the widest spectrum by protecting families from intruders. Even if the electrical power goes out, the family dog still knows a burglar is out there. Burglars

69

do not trust a vicious and crazy dog in close quarters. Their residential break-in comes to a halt the moment the dog attacks. The thieves are now on the defensive – running for their lives. In any event, secrecy is lost, the chance of being caught rises, and it is no surprise that a dog's bark, itself, deters crime.

(b) Strong cat idea
For some people, public health is a bigger issue than public safety. These folks suggest that cats provide the superior benefit of eliminating an unsanitary rat population.

(c) The replacement
However, this argument overlooks the fact that a simple purchase of rat poison at the store for $18 will eliminate rats, while there is no low cost way of keeping intruders from breaking into one's home the way a dog does. Given that there are low cost ways to achieve the benefits of cats while few, if any expensive technologies can replace dogs, it is clear that dogs deliver superior value to the public good."

There is some risk to the replacement approach. It is a value judgment on our part. We choose which idea is <u>better</u> than the opposition's <u>good</u> idea. While proofreading this section of the manuscript, my sister reminded me that when we were two and three years old respectively, we had eaten some rat poison that we discovered under the kitchen sink. We were rushed to the hospital in a helpful neighbor's Mercedes, we toddlers throwing up along the way to the embarrassment of our mother. Upon arrival at the hospital, my sister and I suffered the ultimate humiliation of having our stomachs pumped. This childhood experience illustrates the more risky nature of the Replacement Approach© vis-à-vis the Direct Approach© – we do not know the opinion of our reader/grader such as my sister on the subject of rat poison as a household rodent deterrent. However, the Direct Approach© is not always available to us, while the Replacement Approach© always is. Additionally, it is fun to execute because replacing provides a wide-open assortment of defuse choices while simultaneously removing the sting of a dangerous counter idea.

STRATEGY TOOL #5: Defuse with The Replacement Approach© by presenting a better idea in place of the opposing strength.

Benefits of Defusing

The value of defusing is that we show our teacher skills that are on her list of things we must do to get an A. For essay tests, our teacher's list includes:
- Recalling key information
- Considering multiple options
- Weighing the strengths and weaknesses of those options
- Drawing reasonable conclusions based upon our analysis

While the grader may not personally agree with our stand, as a professional educator, she will admire and value a soundly thought out piece of writing. True teachers are empowering us to think and communicate. They will reward us for these skills. Even teachers with a personal agenda are affected by persuasive defuses. In the end, we achieve the following benefits anytime we execute a **defuse**:
- Gaining the initiative
- Interrupting the graders' skeptical thoughts
- Taking out an opposing point of view
- Earning a higher grade or winning a scholarship

Choosing the "Other Side"

We have now arrived at an enviable position. We can now argue either side – if we choose to. We have the ability to write a convincing essay about cats or about dogs. This freedom would never have been possible if we had not done our THINKING first. Imagine how deflated we would be if we wrote an entire essay about dogs and realized in the process, that cats were the better choice? Instead, by building a T-View Outline©, we have in effect, waved our magic wand, altered time, gone into the future and seen what the end result looks like.

Which one should we choose? Well, we weigh the sides against each other by putting each stack of ideas on an imaginary scale and ask, *"Which side is heavier?"* We look at the left, and ask, *"Can I argue this dog list of ideas*

convincingly?" Then we look at the right and ask a similar question *"Can I argue this cat list of ideas convincingly?"* Then we ask, *"Which one is going to be the strongest?"* Our goal is to write the most convincing essay because it will give us the best chance of a higher grade. Remember, school is a game. When we sense that the other side has a stronger case, it is time to switch sides.

> **PERFORMANCE SECRET #8:   Choose the "other" side when it delivers a more persuasive argument.**

Throughout our dialogue we have been assuming that we are going to write about dogs, so right now, dogs seems to be the obvious choice. However, there is also a strong case for cats. We present both essays to the reader later on, the "Dog is Better" essay, **Roll Over, Fluffy!**, starts on page 157 while the "Cat is Better" Essay, **Cats Rule, Dogs Drool**, starts on page 160. Feel free to browse ahead and read both of them. Make sure you return to this page, as we will continue to reveal the process for writing a high scoring essay starting on the next page.

Step One of our Game Plan, THINK, is now complete. In the next section, we will organize our thinking so that we can WRITE in a smooth flow. We call Step 2, our organizing step, STAGING.

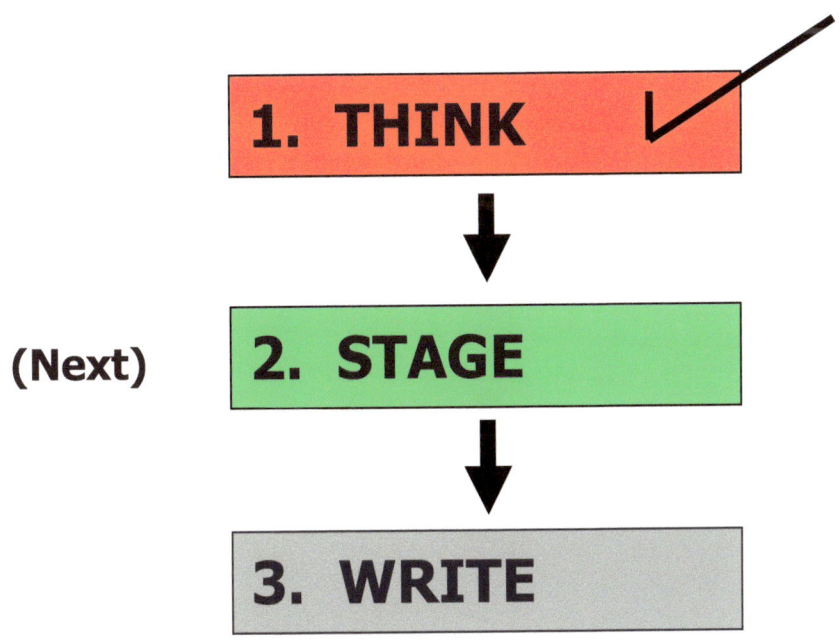

2. STAGE

> **2. STAGE:**
> 2-A. **Write Thesis Statement**
> 2-B. **Sequence Ideas**
> 2-C. **Divide Time**

In this section, you will learn the secrets to:
- ***Write a thesis statement that works***
- ***Know what to keep in and leave out***
- ***Put ideas in the best order***
- ***Leverage time to your advantage***

Staging is the middle step in our 3-step process for writing essays. Recall that our Game Plan is THINK – STAGE – WRITE. Staging is the shortest step, while happily being the most powerful way to improve our grades with the least effort. If there is one thing that separates those who are "smart" in school from those who are not, it is how the "smart" people stage their ideas, write from a clear plan and use time to their advantage.

Surfing

Surfing is an adventure that requires advance preparation. One simply does not decide to go surfing spontaneously. An enjoyable experience requires the right destination, proper equipment and accurate timing. A trip starts days before, as we prepare our tools and equipment: selecting the perfect surfboard, waxing it, finding a wetsuit that fits and commandeering a vehicle that can handle our board. No two beaches are the same, so we choose a beach with waves that match our skill level. Lastly, there is timing. Mother Nature plays a decisive role in our enjoyment. Once we are ready, we watch the wave conditions. This requires an internet site, weather channel, or a home close enough to see the waves. The waves must be high enough, but not too high!

Transportation

Destination

Equipment - Wetsuit

Equipment - Surf Board

Timing

Here is a list of items that I have found to be indispensable:
- Surf Board
- Wet Suit
- Towel
- Swim Suit
- Sunscreen
- Sports Drink
- Transportation
- Beach
- Real-time status of wave conditions

Notice how much is required before we are ready to surf. Once prepared, we wait for acceptable wave conditions to present themselves. Then we head out to the beach. The surfer prepares everything in advance, before he leaves for the beach. There is a name for this type of behavior. It is called staging. **Staging is the act of placing everything in order beforehand, so that when we actually do the activity, our actions flow smoothly and effortlessly.**

Imagine the despair of showing up at the beach and discovering that the ocean is as calm as a bathtub. Likewise, imagine showing up without a wet suit in cold water. How do we feel when leaving the sunscreen at home only to find that there is not a cloud in the sky? These mental mistakes result in either, a miserable time freezing in the water or scorching sunburn in the evening. Interestingly, no true surfer considers any of these staging activities an inconvenience. She enjoys the gathering of the items and watching the wave conditions because she has mastered PERFORMANCE SECRET #1: View surfing as a game. Love the adventure of playing that game.

Surfers demonstrate three aspects of staging. They combine a destination, equipment and timing. Coincidentally, the staging of an essay requires preparation in the same three areas:

	Surfing	**Essay Exams**
Destination	The Beach	Thesis Statement
Equipment	Board & Wetsuit	T-View Outline©
Timing	Catching the Wave	Timing Ladder©

STAGING is the action that makes all of our THINKING pay off. A fully staged essay includes:
1. **Thesis statement**
2. **T-View Outline©**
3. **Timing Ladder©**

In practice, staging an essay can take seconds or minutes depending on our individual capabilities and the requirements of the essay. As we learn to STAGE before we WRITE, we shift from a survival mode into a thriving mode. Starting with all the tools in place makes the actual writing of the essay easy. The major difference between studying and performing is the amount of effort that we expend writing our essay. STAGING separates out the task of organizing of our ideas from the heavy lifting (THINKING) and the physical expenditure (WRITING). The benefit of doing this step correctly is that we are free to write our essay quickly and smoothly. The result is a higher scoring essay. Meanwhile, the study people simply take no thought beforehand to what they will write and just "wing it" – with haphazard results.

2-A. Write Your Thesis Statement

Why we have Thesis Statements

There is a popular saying in use today *"you never have a second chance to make a first impression."* The purpose of a thesis statement is similar to the importance of making a good first impression. The longer our essay goes on without the reader knowing our purpose, the worse we look as a writer and the lower our grade goes.

Therefore, we could say that our job is to give the reader a complete idea of where we are going as early as humanly possible. The more quickly our reader knows our intention, the sooner he can relax and listen to our message. When we keep the reader/grader in the dark, he attempts to figure out what we are going to prove rather than focusing on how we are proving it. The more confused our grader gets, the lower our grade becomes. In this chapter on staging, we learn how to write a thesis that leaves no doubt as to where we are going.

The idea of a thesis has been around for thousands of years. The ancient Greeks gave us the word, and today it has become a universal convention for telling a reader what we are going to say. The definition of a thesis is – a proposition to be proved or an argument to be forwarded.

While the word "thesis" usually refers to a whole paper and "thesis statement" to one sentence, we will use both terms in this book to mean the same thing: a point of view we are proving. It is important to realize, that our essay is not a conversation about something. It is a conversation proving a point of view, delivering a message and taking a stand. We should be comfortable with that. Under the First Amendment of the Constitution of the United States, we are given the right to speak our mind and a thesis statement is a sentence that expresses our unique insight on a question, issue or principle.

Let the Ideas Guide the Thesis

Once we have built a list of ideas both pro and con, we allow our ideas to show us the way to the thesis. The answer lays somewhere in the two lists, either Dogs Best or Cats Best. Looking at the Dog's Best list, we wonder which pro-dog idea is invincible over cats, so we ask, *"What is the one aspect for which cats have no answer?"* Looking across the vertical line, we see that it is "Trainable." Cats have no match for this. Further confirmation comes as we realize that "Trainable" is the feature that makes most of the other ideas for dogs possible. Our thesis statement flows from this observation:

"Dogs deliver superior value to society over cats because people can train them to follow spoken commands."

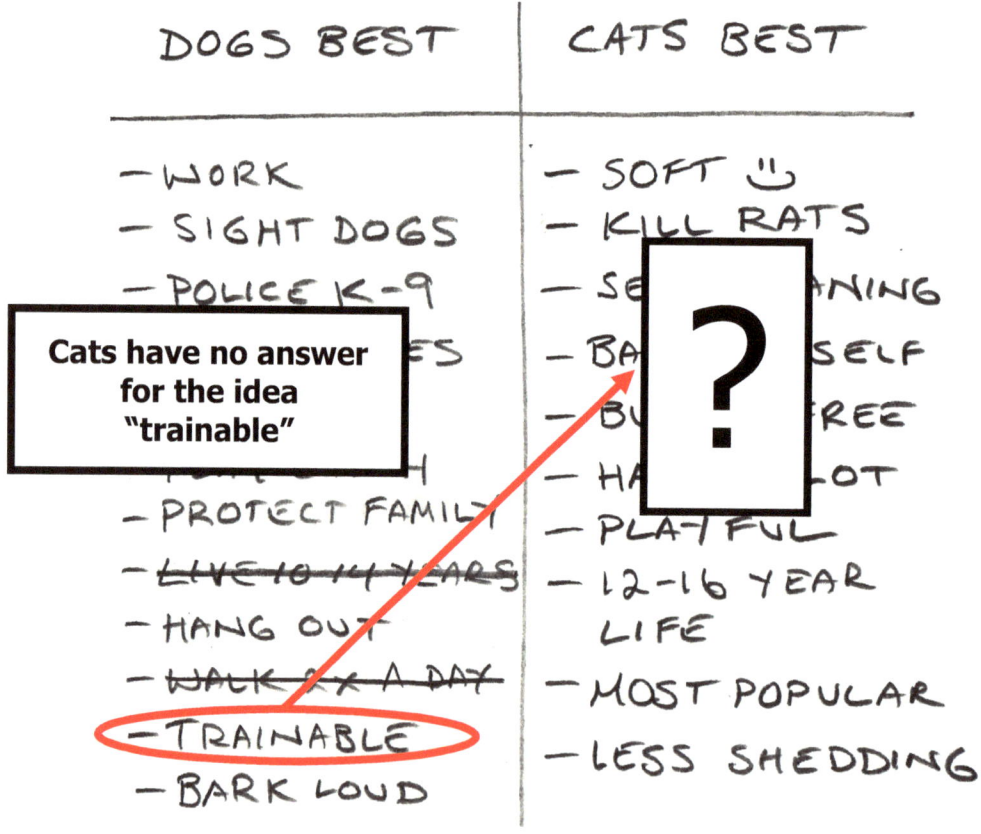

PERFORMANCE SECRET #9: Allow the ideas to show the way to your thesis. Find the invincible idea and use it as the foundation for your thesis.

The Single-Thought Thesis© Technique

Common sense would lead one to believe, given the choice, that we would write our thesis so that every grader would understand what we mean to say. Unfortunately, many of us have written convoluted statements in the past that lowered our grade. Worse yet, we may have gone on to write an essay that strayed far from our thesis statement. Fortunately, when we allow our ideas to guide our thesis and then write a clear and simple thesis statement – we avoid both of the tendencies mentioned in this paragraph.

If there were different ways to say our thesis, ideally we would choose the most simple and short expression of it. The secret to achieving this is to write a thesis that we can <u>describe</u> in a <u>single</u> <u>thought</u>.

Here is a sample thesis for **Dogs vs. Cats** described in a single thought:
1. *"Dogs deliver superior value to society over cats because people can train them to follow spoken commands."*
[Good – Single-Thought Thesis©, trainable]

We might be tempted to write one with more "weight" in it, as follows:
2. *Dogs deliver superior value to society over cats because dogs perform tasks in the work place, guide handicapped people and provide companionship to millions of members of society, while cats often run wild in the neighborhood, kill harmless birds and ignore people in their own homes.*
[Bad – providing the reasons, not the insight or idea]

We might be tempted to be brief and enthusiastic:
3. *Dogs are smart, quick learning, obedient and loyal animals, therefore, dogs deliver superior value to society over cats.*
[Bad – going in too many directions at once]

Choice #1 keeps our reader focused on exactly what we will prove, that dogs are better <u>because we can train them</u>. The reader now has a sense for our insight and the idea we will prove. She may think *"Gee that is interesting, I wonder how you [the student] are going to pull this off?"* Meanwhile, #2 is the proof for dogs rather than the idea and #3 opens up multiple reasons to prove, not a single thesis.

It does not matter how complex or elegant our position is. We can always refine any idea down to a single thought. In essay **I. What Ancient Rome**

Could Teach Romeo and Juliet (page 172) the student writes, *"If Romeo and Juliet had been honest, they would have lived."* This is a Single-Thought Thesis©.

Taking the time to filter our thinking down to a single thought is what professional writers do, and is one of the main reasons why we take a few moments to THINK before we WRITE. It is the act of going from foggy to clear. Getting to the source of our thinking puts us in the mode of great writers. Teachers reward us for brilliant writing or anything that comes close to it. They are passionate about language and admire writing that that has original insights and describes those insights clearly.

PERFORMANCE SECRET #10: Use the Single-Thought Thesis© technique to simplify your thesis down to one thought.

Often, the first time we think of our thesis, it is in a simple form. Then we quickly start to improve it, expand it and find better ways to say it. The tendency is to second-guess ourselves and complicate the wording. This typically results in a thesis that is worse than the one we started with. Rather than expand the thesis beyond a single thought, we should save those ideas for use later in our essay as we seek to describe, prove and share the impact of our thesis.

The <u>moment</u> we can <u>express</u> our <u>thesis</u> in a <u>single</u> <u>thought</u>, we know that we are at the <u>core</u> of our <u>argument</u>. If our core is strong, and we focus all of our ideas around it, we will write an impressive essay.

Be Confident

At this point it is appropriate to take a "commercial break" to chat about the frame of mind we get to be in if we are to play a winning game. Our attitude about writing our essay affects our grade more than any other aspect of our game. We may be able to convince ourselves that we are confident and positive, but if deep down we are not, the reader will see through our facade. The reader sees our attitude in the words we choose and the tone of voice we use. How do we feel? What is our attitude about our teacher? This subject? Life in general? Our attitude will come through our writing just as surely as every word we speak comes through with an underlying tone of voice.

Being confident is the most important attitude to radiate through our writing. The teacher has brought us in, as it were on a talk show, to ask our opinion on the subject. Because of these circumstances, while we are writing our essay, we are the expert. Experts share their own opinions based upon their own unique thoughts. Therefore, a clear straightforward essay is more effective than one that attempts to agree with multiple points of view. Let's leave talking out of both sides of one's mouth to politicians, our job is to communicate our personal ideas clearly. We do this by being confident and sticking to one story.

I once read an article in an airline magazine about survival tips for the first-time college student. The author had interviewed professors about how students could avoid the most common mistakes freshmen make when writing papers. One English teacher shared the sentence that annoys him the most: *"It's not for me to say."* His smart response in red ink is always, *"if it's not for you to say, then whose is it?"* When we are answering an essay question, it <u>is</u> our <u>right</u> to <u>make</u> <u>conclusions</u>, <u>recommend</u> <u>changes</u> and <u>identify</u> <u>solutions</u> that will make the world a better place – or at least answer the teacher's question. We are more persuasive when we state our position exactly the way it is rather than make it fuzzy to avoid hurting someone else's feelings. We receive full credit for clear and focused thinking. Remember, we are the expert. Be confident. This confidence starts with a Single-Thought Thesis©, such as:

"Dogs deliver superior value to society over cats because people can train them to follow spoken commands"

2-B. Sequence Our Ideas

The Flexibility of the T-View Outline©

Surfers look at the ocean conditions and visualize what it will be like to ride those waves before they decide to jump in the water. Similarly, we can look at the different ways to present our ideas, choose the one that works best, and see it before we write it. With the T-View Outline© we work in the moldable clay of our ideas before they harden (write the essay).

Sequence is the aspect of presentation we focus on first. We start by attempting to number the ideas in the order that makes the most sense. In **Dogs vs. Cats**, we mentally number the ideas from 1-10 for dogs. If the flow works well in our mind, we then number them in pen or pencil as shown inside the red circle below. Now we recheck the flow of ideas in our mind. If a different order makes more sense, we can simply scratch out and renumber the ideas. Notice that we are changing the sequence of our ideas at the speed of thought. This flexibility and speed is light years ahead of changing our direction while writing. The difference is that before, the order of our ideas was based upon when they popped into our head as we wrote. **Now, the order of our ideas is the most convincing order.**

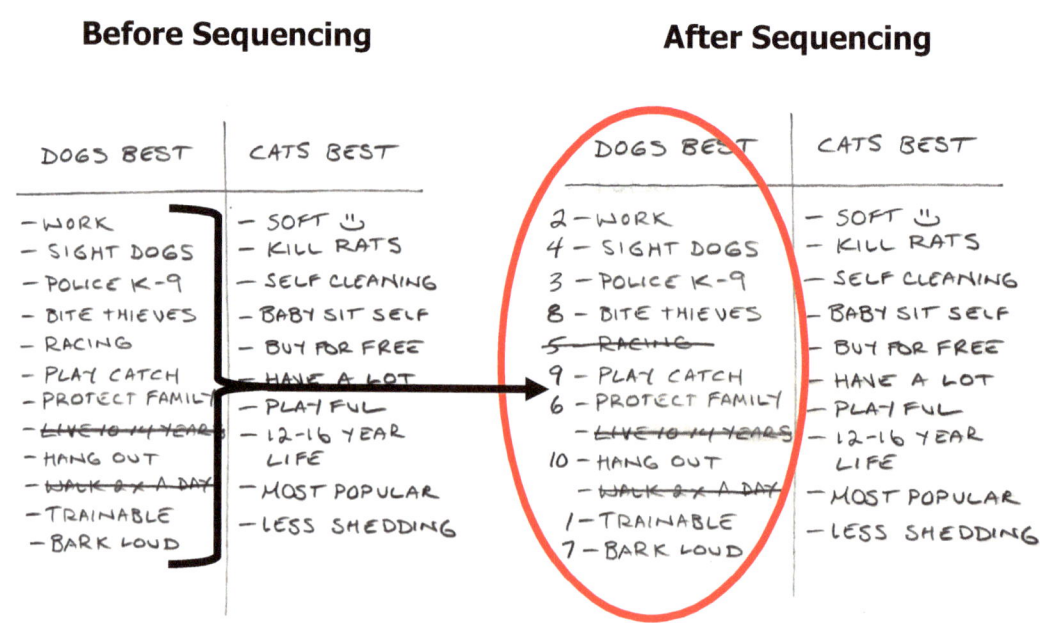

When we present thoughts in a powerful logical order, we just look smarter. The smarter we look the better grade we earn!

Sequencing Options – Two Roads

The most obvious question now is, *"What is the most convincing order?"* In other words, *"How would we even know?"* Questions such as these often tempt us to gather all the different ways we could sequence our ideas. Then we could assess each and pick the best one, making sure not to miss any. Figuring out all the ways is unnecessary because there are only two powerful ways to order the presentation of our ideas.

The first is in order of strength. An order of strength goes from strongest to weakest, or weakest to strongest. The other order is one that tells a story by building one idea upon another. Strongest to weakest describes a hierarchy characterized by strength. Weakest to strongest describes a crescendo building up to a climax. A story uses one event to set up the next event and so on until we reach a conclusion in thought. A story must have at least a beginning, middle and an end to make that journey in thought. We will call these two sequences:

- **Hierarchy of Strength**
- **Building Upon Prior Ideas**

Both of these strategies are effective. The best choice depends upon the situation. We will now look at where each approach fits best.

Hierarchy of Strength

Hierarchies exist in many aspects of life for the purpose of order and control. For example, an army assigns leaders to different commands by their rank so that it is clear who takes orders from whom. There is always one person higher than another until we reach the Commander in Chief, the President of the United States. Card games rank every card from top to bottom starting at Ace, King, Queen, Jack, 10, 9, 8, 7 and so forth. Higher-ranking cards control lower ranking cards. Sports teams assign a captain on offense and a captain on defense to interact with the referees. Organizations who use hierarchies achieve objectives faster because they execute with order and effectiveness.

How do we use this phenomenon of hierarchies in our essay writing? When making a case for our thesis, we use our strongest ideas first to influence the viewpoint of our grader. A hierarchy of strength is the <u>preferred</u> <u>approach</u> when we have <u>one</u> or <u>two</u> <u>ideas</u> that are <u>significantly</u> <u>more</u> <u>convincing</u> than the <u>other</u> <u>ideas</u> we will present. By starting with the stronger ones first, we deliver a more persuasive argument on a logical and emotional level.

As we consider this strategy, we see three positive results. The first plays into the psychology of the grader. If the initial idea makes a strong impact and convinces the grader that our thesis is valid, she will read the remaining weaker ideas with this positively skewed view. The lesser ideas, in effect, appear stronger than they really are because they are associated with the first ideas in the hierarchy. The second result is pure efficiency. If we run short of time and have to shut down our essay in a hurry, we already have put down enough proof on paper to make our case. In a time-constrained situation, we have made the most effective use of limited words. The third benefit is protection against lazy graders. If the grader is going to start skimming our essay after she gets the general direction of our thoughts and writing capabilities, and we have led with our best idea first, the grader will grasp our best idea regardless of how much more she reads. Consequently, we have maximized our chance to get a high grade.

Our first paragraph in **Roll Over, Fluffy!**, page 157, presents the strongest idea why dogs deliver more value than cats – dogs can be trained by talking to them:

Among domesticated animals, dogs uniquely possess the ability to be trained by verbal commands to perform specific tasks. As a result, we find people in society training dogs commercially and privately. Commercially, police dogs are trained as puppies to follow the commands: sit, down, stay, heel and come here. Later, as adults, these dogs are trained to attack criminals and retreat, sniff out weapons and drugs, and detain suspects.

Now we will show how to design a Hierarchy of Strength with the **Dogs vs. Cats** essay by numbering the ideas from strongest to weakest.

DOGS BEST	CATS BEST
2 – WORK	– SOFT ☺
4 – SIGHT DOGS	– KILL RATS
3 – POLICE K-9	– SELF CLEANING
8 – BITE THIEVES	– BABY SIT SELF
5 – RACING	– ~~BUY FOR FREE~~
9 – ~~PLAY CATCH~~	
6 – PROTECT FAMILY	
– ~~LIVE 10-14 YEARS~~	– 12-16 YEAR LIFE
10 – HANG OUT	
– ~~WALK 2X A DAY~~	– MOST POPULAR
1 – TRAINABLE	– LESS SHEDDING
7 – BARK LOUD	

Sequence Ideas from Strongest to Weakest!

We know that "Trainable" is our strongest idea, and "Hang out" is our weakest. So we can number them 1 and 10 and then start working the middle. I decided to present my ideas in the following order: 1-Trainable, 2-Work, 3-Police K-9, 4-Sight Dogs, 5-Racing, 6-Protect the Home, 7-Bark Loud and 8-Bite Thieves. Why is *RACING* before Protect Home? More training is involved with *RACING* than a dog's natural instinct. We complete our essay by 9-Play catch and 10-Hang out.

PERFORMANCE SECRET #11: Use the Hierarchy of Strength to achieve maximum persuasive impact. Present ideas in declining order, strongest first to weakest last.

Building upon Prior Ideas

When some "if-then" reasoning or story telling is required to prove a thesis, we use the Building upon Prior Ideas strategy. To illustrate, imagine being in a Criminology Class. A bank robbery was committed by blasting the vault door open with explosives. All the safe deposit boxes are empty and valuables taken. We find out through our investigation that a person bought the type of explosives used to blow open the vault a few days before the crime was committed, so we make her a prime suspect. Do we conclude that she is guilty with a single fact? Not yet, we need more than capability. We need to place the suspect at the scene of the crime. Then we discover the suspect's fingerprints inside the vault. Do we conclude that the suspect stole the money? Not yet; she could have been in the vault for a legitimate purpose. We now exclude all the valid reasons for being there. Does she rent a safe deposit box inside? No. Is she a bank employee? No. Does she work for the company that repairs the vault? No. Does she work for the armored transport company that services the bank? No. Once we have ruled out all the possible valid reasons for leaving fingerprints in the vault, we are ready to make our decision: the prime suspect had no reason to be inside the vault except to steal its contents. We can now build our case that the suspect is guilty by building one idea upon the other.

1st idea – Prime suspect bought explosives
2nd idea – Vault door was blown open with the same type of explosives
3rd idea – Prime suspect's fingerprints are inside the vault
4th idea – Prime suspect had no reason to be in the vault

Consider that we could build the ideas above in a 4-1-2-3 sequence and maintain a chronological order by which the crime was committed, but a 3-2-1-4 does not make sense because one has to buy explosives before she can blow the door open and the door must be open before she can put her fingerprints in the vault. Common sense order makes the Building upon Prior Ideas strategy a persuasive one.

Another execution of this strategy is to use a story to illustrate each idea. Each story then becomes an idea that builds on the idea of the prior story until we lead the reader's thought process to a conclusion. Here we are simply switching out an idea, with an entire story that communicates that idea. An example of this strategy appears in Essay III, **Risk** (pages 180-181), where the first two story/ideas set up the significance of the last story/idea. There are three story/ideas presented in the essay to guide the reader's thoughts.

- 1st idea is that someone did not risk and spent the rest of their life married to someone they did not love. (bad result)
- 2nd idea is that someone did take a risk and won a battle that led to ultimate victory and preservation of freedom. (good result)

- 3rd idea is a situation that occurs in the present with an unknown final result. A student must choose to take a risk or not. The first story presented the bad result of not taking a risk. The second story presented the good result of taking a risk. These two stories at the opposite ends of the risk spectrum set up the question posed by the third story, *"Should we take risks?"* The results of the first two story/ideas suggested that taking risks pays off, which now positions the conclusion of the third story and the entire essay to arrive at the only acceptable conclusion – take the risk!

The difference between writing an essay with a random presentation of ideas verses a calculated sequence of ideas is the difference between receiving a "C" grade or an "A" grade for an essay written on the same subject by the same student with the same thesis.

PERFORMANCE SECRET #12: Use the Building Upon Prior Ideas sequence when one idea requires an idea established before it, or when proof depends upon chronological order of ideas.

Focus on the Best Arguments

When grading our papers, teachers are looking for our ability to know the difference between what is important and what is not important. It is important to use ideas that move our argument and proof forward. It is not important to include weak ideas simply to fill up space. Weak ideas dilute the power of our argument and lower our grade. One way an idea can be weak is when it has both positive and negative aspects. In **Dogs vs. Cats**, *RACING* is one such idea. While greyhounds and whippets demonstrate how versatile dogs' learning capabilities are and provide the social value of entertainment, the *RACING* activity they are involved in includes gambling. Since our question focuses on social value, this idea could either help our cause or hurt it – depending on the opinion of our grader on gambling. Since we don't know our grader's opinion, we cross *RACING* off the list and leave it out altogether. Our goal is to score the most grade points. Therefore, we always advance the strength of our thesis by focusing on our best arguments and avoiding weak ones.

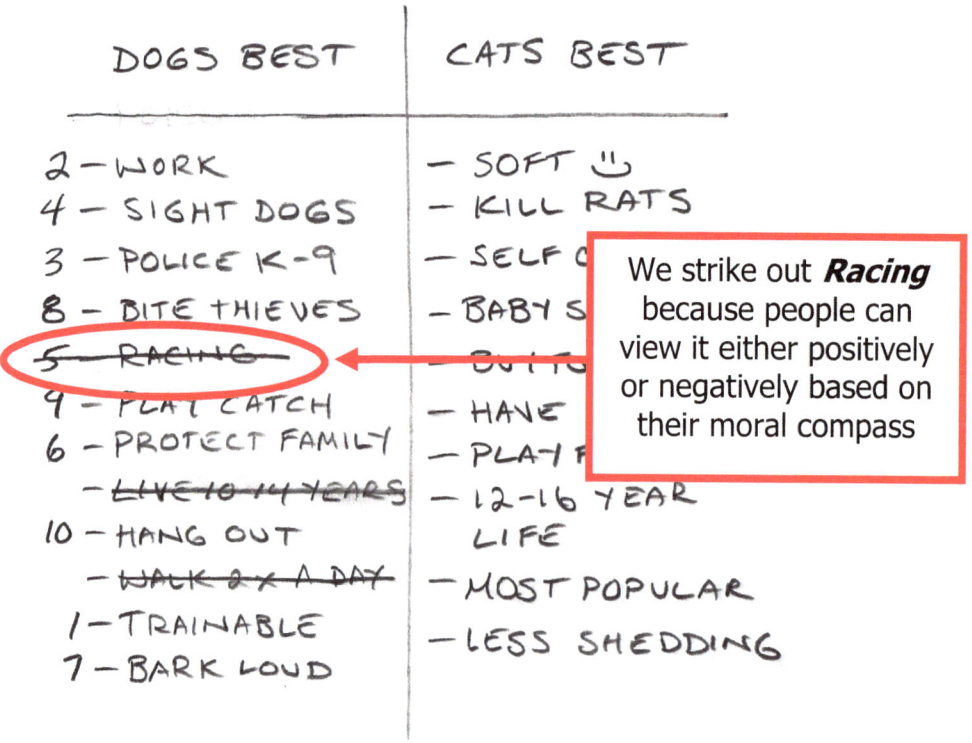

We strike out **Racing** because people can view it either positively or negatively based on their moral compass

---

PERFORMANCE SECRET #13: If an idea does not advance the strength of your thesis – toss it out!

The Idea Stack©

Now that we have decided which ideas are in and which are out, it makes sense to view our ideas as a unit. Soon our flow of thought will focus on the structure of our essay. Our ideas are merely a piece of the structure. Since our ideas will be easier to work with when we group them together as one thing, we shall call our list an Idea Stack© throughout the remainder of this book.

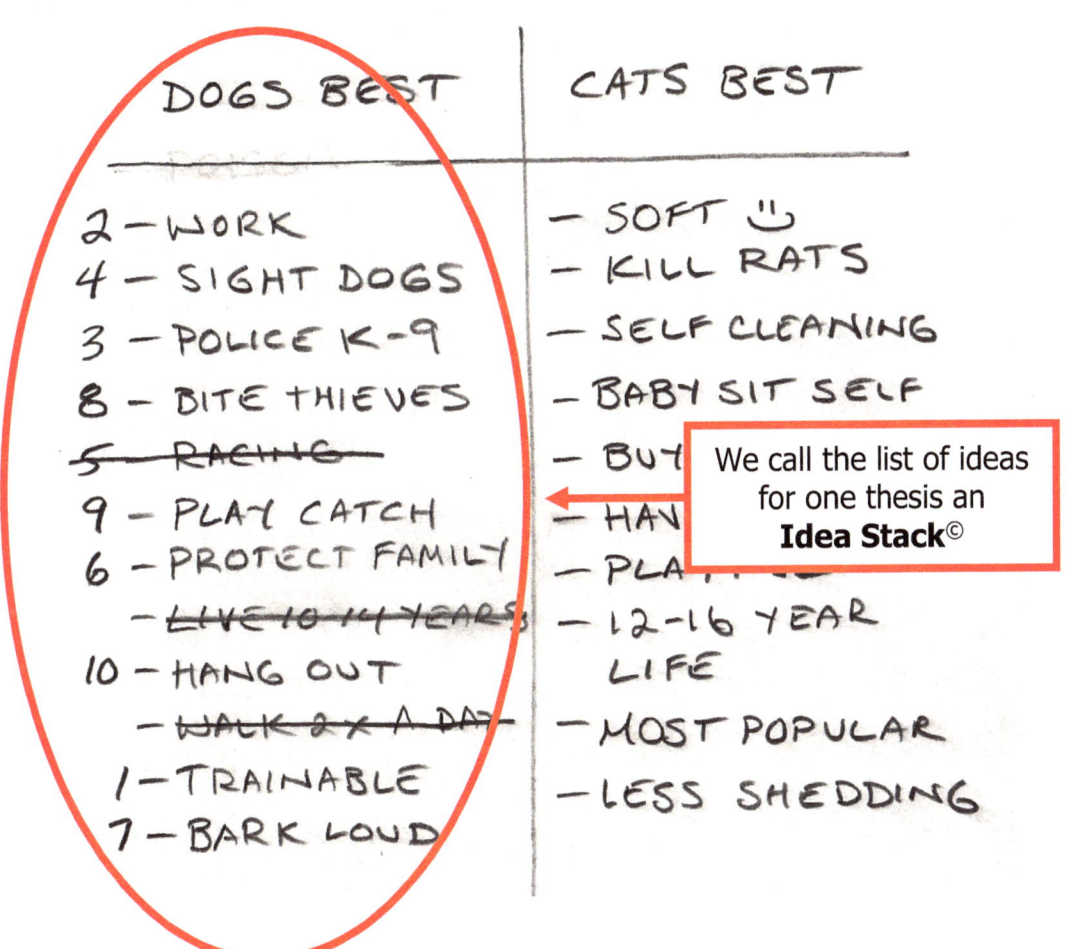

We call the list of ideas for one thesis an **Idea Stack©**

Now that we have our Idea Stack© perfected, we may be tempted to start writing our essay. We can do this. However, if we do, we will not have planned how to manage our time. Since the use of our time often makes or breaks our grade, we will perform one more STAGING activity – maximizing our time, with a tool we call the Timing Ladder©.

2-C. Timing Ladder©

Positioning Ourselves for Success

Information, Location and Time are the three elements we balance while writing an essay. How many of us think about time as we write? Those of us who do not are missing an opportunity to get a higher grade.

I once heard a champion basketball player say that he always counted the time on the game clock in his head from the moment the ball came inbounds so that even if he couldn't see the clock, he always knew how much time he had left to shoot. Starting with his back to the basket, he once made the winning shot in a championship game by turning around and letting the ball fly in the last second. The ball was in the air when the clock went to zero – but it still counted. The opposition had no time left to respond. The game was over. Herein lies one secret of a champion; he was counting time as he played. His counting shows that winners always know exactly where they are in their game.

Right now, while we are in the STAGE phase, it is valuable to plan our use of time so that we can blend **information** and **location** together effectively. We will present detailed models to show how to allocate time. The models illustrate the application of math and fractions. How you apply the numbers and fractions in a test situation is up to you.

How do we learn to use time to our advantage? Well, we start with a small step; master it and then add another step and master that and so on until we are using a complete approach. One way to start counting time is to set aside the last two minutes of each essay for writing the conclusion. We do this by making a rule for ourselves that says –

No matter where we are in the essay, when we hit the two-minute mark; we finish writing the current sentence with the shortest thought (we shut it down), and then we start a new paragraph – the conclusion.

Once we have added this basic step to our game, we add more rules one-by-one until we are consistently finishing on time while presenting all of our ideas. At this performance level, we have mastered our metaphor on page four, **"don't stop until you get to the other side."**

Divide Time into Two Blocks

We now look at how to leverage our time. It starts with knowing <u>when</u> to stop preparing and <u>when</u> to start writing. Note that this is a single moment in time. Knowing when to start writing gives us the freedom during a test to THINK and STAGE without stress.

Now it just comes down to blocking out time. The preparing block includes both THINK/STAGE while the writing block is WRITE. We imagine the moment when we switch tasks as simply being where we cut the rectangle of total time in two. We assign the number 1 for <u>THINKING/STAGING</u> and the number 2 for <u>WRITING</u>. We have now built a model in our mind, as shown below:

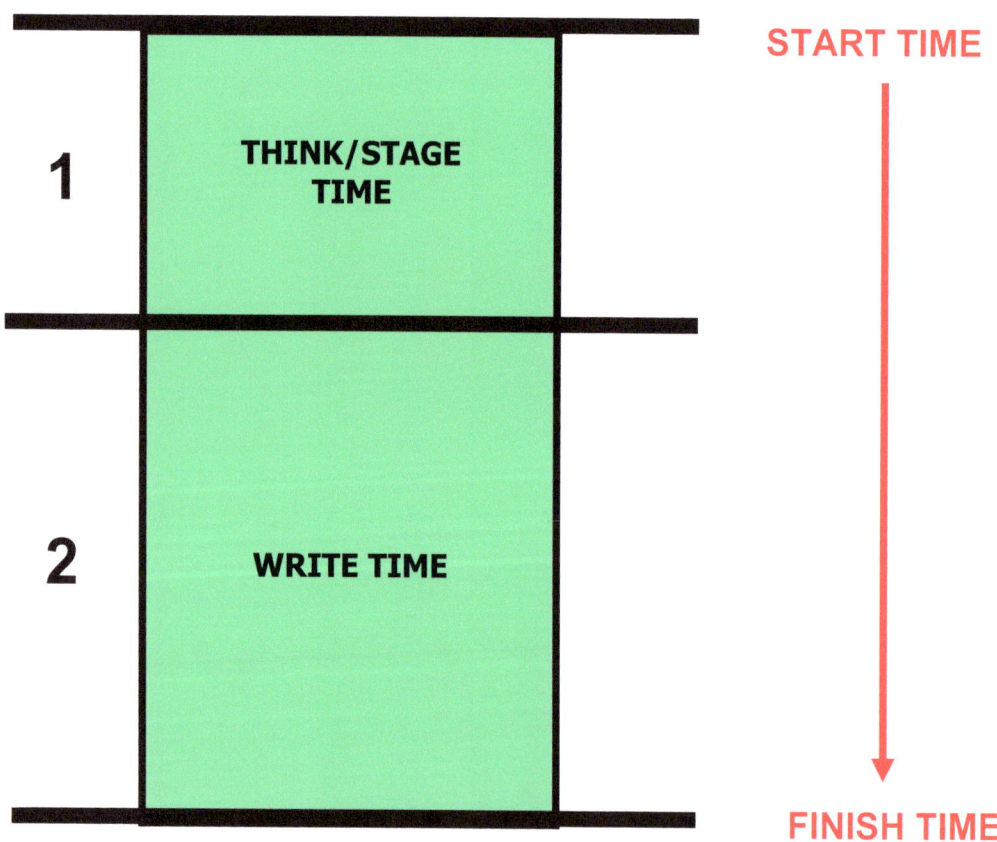

Time occurs in the direction from top to bottom as shown with the red arrow to the right of the diagram. The downward flow makes sense bearing in mind that time flows in the same direction that we write – from beginning to end. The three horizontal black lines, with a little imagination, appear as rungs on a ladder. The rungs mark our steps through time, Start-Shift-Stop, a visual picture that spawns the name Timing Ladder©.

During our first block of time, we are jotting down our ideas and numbering them. Although the time expended to do this is priceless, we still get to be smart about it. It would be bad to be thinking when time runs out – having written nothing. On the other hand, it would be bad to write a disorganized and confusing essay – having put no thought behind it. Personally, I found the balance of preparation vs. writing to be between a short block of 1/5th time (20%) to a long block of 1/3rd time (33%) for Thinking/Staging. The following table gives the student an idea of how much time these fractions mean in minutes:

Total Minutes for Question	1/5th Block Thinking/Staging	1/4th Block Thinking/Staging	1/3rd Block Thinking/Staging
10	2 minutes	3 minutes	3 minutes
15	3 minutes	4 minutes	5 minutes
20	4 minutes	5 minutes	7 minutes
25	5 minutes	6 minutes	8 minutes
30	6 minutes	8 minutes	10 minutes

During a live test, we simply round the numbers to make the math easy. Mathematical accuracy is not the goal here, balancing our time into two blocks is. For example, 1/4th of the time on a 15-minute question rounds 3.75 to 4 minutes. There is no need to memorize this chart. Simply remember that the key to dividing time into two blocks is to keep the math easy. Pick a time and run with it.

Once I believed that thinking before you write paid off, I allocated a third of my time to Thinking/Staging on a final exam in graduate school. The actual notes from these 15 minutes of prep time appear on page 189, following Essay V, **New Airport in Chicago**. It is only through setting aside time to THINK and then using it effectively to plan our essay, that we are going to achieve a grade at the top of our potential.

PERFORMANCE SECRET #14: Split time into two blocks:
   1 - THINK/STAGE
   2 - WRITE

Link Tasks to the Clock

Once we are masters at balancing two blocks of time, 1-THINK/STAGE and 2-WRITE, we can improve our time management skills. The strategy is to pace the writing of our Idea Stack© with the clock on the wall. Conceptually, we are going to insert the Idea Stack© between an Introduction and a Conclusion, and then lay that beside the Timing Ladder©. Recall that in **Dogs vs. Cats** we numbered nine (9) ideas for our essay. Each of the white spaces between the black rungs to the right of the Idea Stack© below represents the time set aside to write one of those ideas. We have now divided the time allotted to write our Idea Stack© into nine equal parts.

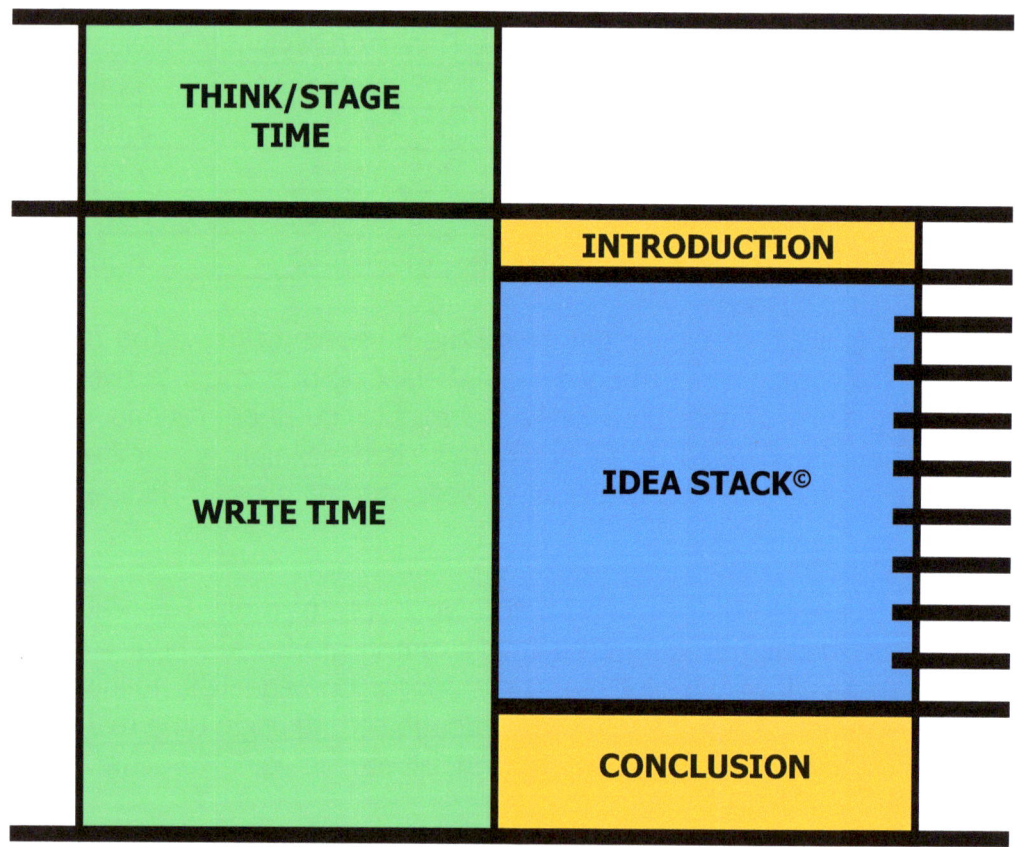

On the next page, we see how our model looks when it is hand written. For this illustration, assume that we have 15 minutes to write our essay. On the left, we break 15 minutes into two blocks:
- **3** minutes for THINK/STAGE
- **12** minutes for WRITE

On the right, we break up our 12 WRITE minutes into
- **1, 9** and **2** for Introduction, Idea Stack© and Conclusion

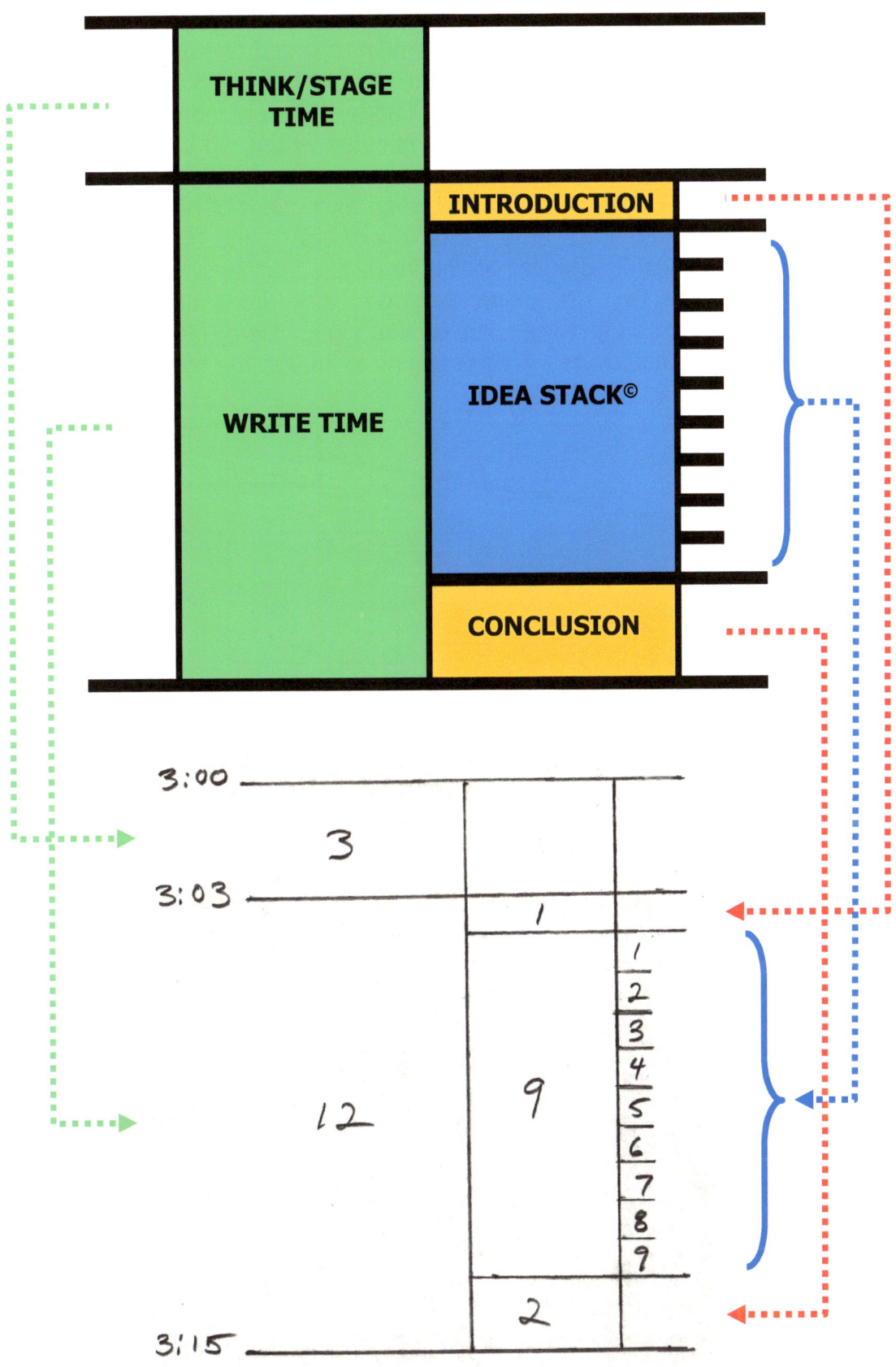

During a live exam, the rungs on our ladder guide us to know when to switch paragraphs or to switch ideas. We plan to spend one minute writing each idea in **Dogs vs. Cats**. Good writing requires smooth transitions, so we take the liberty to follow the rungs of the Timing Ladder© loosely individually but tightly collectively. If we spend one and a half minutes writing an idea, then we must cut back on the next idea by 30 seconds to stay on schedule. In practice, we do not manage every minute; rather we have an awareness of how many ideas we have written and how much time we have expended, and then change speeds accordingly. The goal is to finish writing inside the teacher's "STOP" window. It is highly beneficial to write down the true clock times of key shift points somewhere so that you can see them as you write. Here, after glancing at the wall clock, we see that **Dogs vs. Cats** begins at 3:00 in the afternoon.

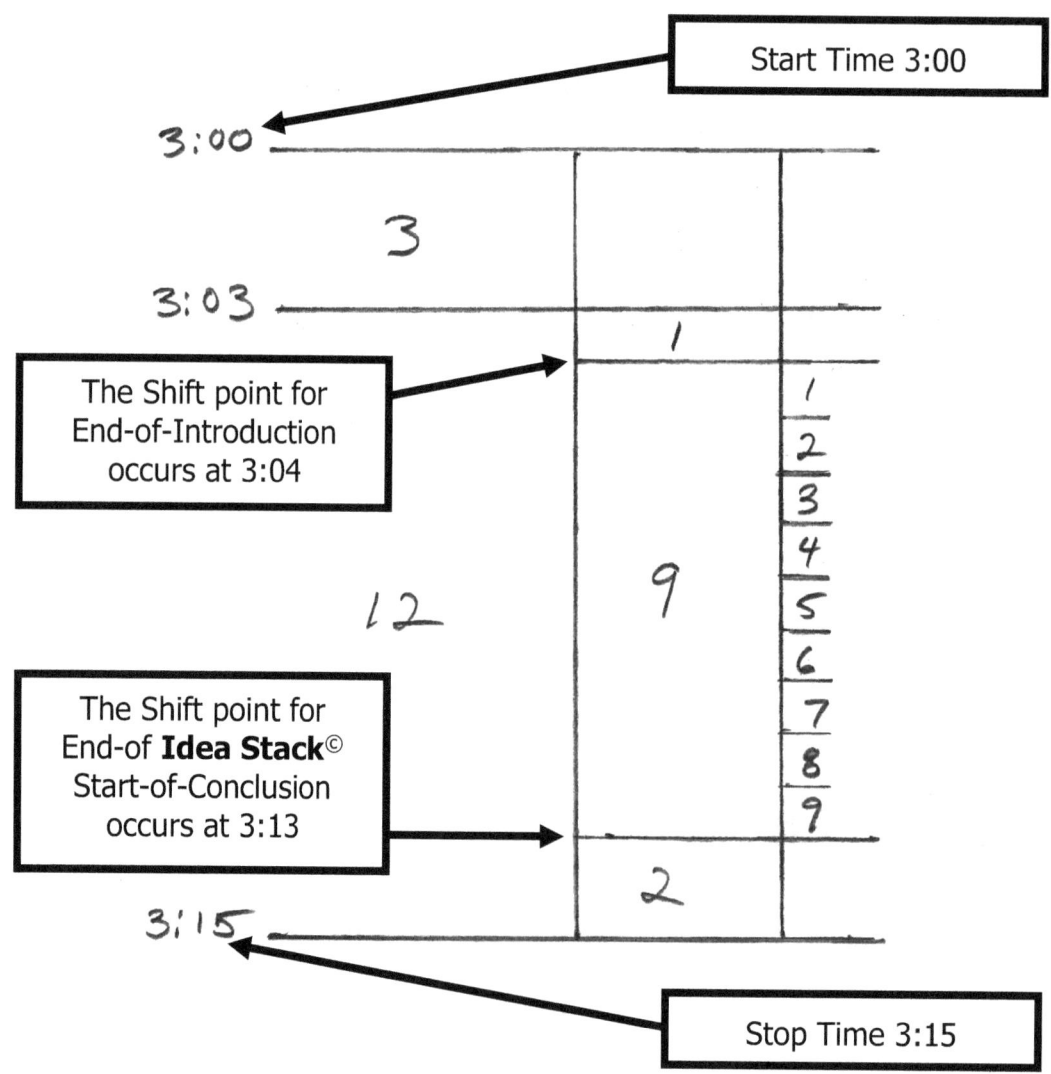

The two most critical times are when we shift from Introduction to Idea Stack© and shift from Idea Stack© to Conclusion. Hitting these points in stride puts our entire essay in balance.

During exams, I often found myself slightly ahead or behind where I planned to be. By being aware of my location in the Timing Ladder© I found that I could push myself to writer faster or relax to slow down. Speeding up means that I figure out how to say the same message with fewer words; slowing down means that I focus on being descriptive and elegant. One can become expert at pacing time and ideas, developing a sixth sense about where one is in an essay and the need to speed up or slow down.

I first developed the Timing Ladder© in my head. Each time I used it, I added to it. Occasionally, I jotted down the numbers such as the 1-9-2 on my test paper off to the side (lightly, so as not to catch the teachers eye). Mostly I found it easier to manage in my head as I wrote. The Timing Ladder© is a concept and each of us has a different grasp of math so feel free to use and express the Timing Ladder© in whatever form works for you.

> **STRATEGY TOOL #6:** Use the Timing Ladder© to know when to start writing, when to switch from one idea to the next, and when to stop writing.

Our teacher's game plan is to give out high grades for clear communication and low grades for scattered communication. With the newfound vision and control of the Timing Ladder©, we start to make calculated decisions about how we express our ideas – either quickly or elegantly. This results in a clear and complete presentation and gives our teacher the evidence he needs to give us a higher grade.

Staging Complete

We have now gathered our Destination, Equipment and Timing in preparation for writing our essay:

Destination	**Single-Thought Thesis©**
Equipment	**T-View Outline© and Idea Stack©**
Timing	**Timing Ladder©**

Fully armed after executing the THINK and STAGE phases, we are now ready to execute the third phase of our Game Plan – WRITE. We are in an envious space. We have surveyed the journey, prepared our equipment and know where we are going to be at all times. Coming up next are the presentation strategies that will set our writing apart from everyone else in the class.

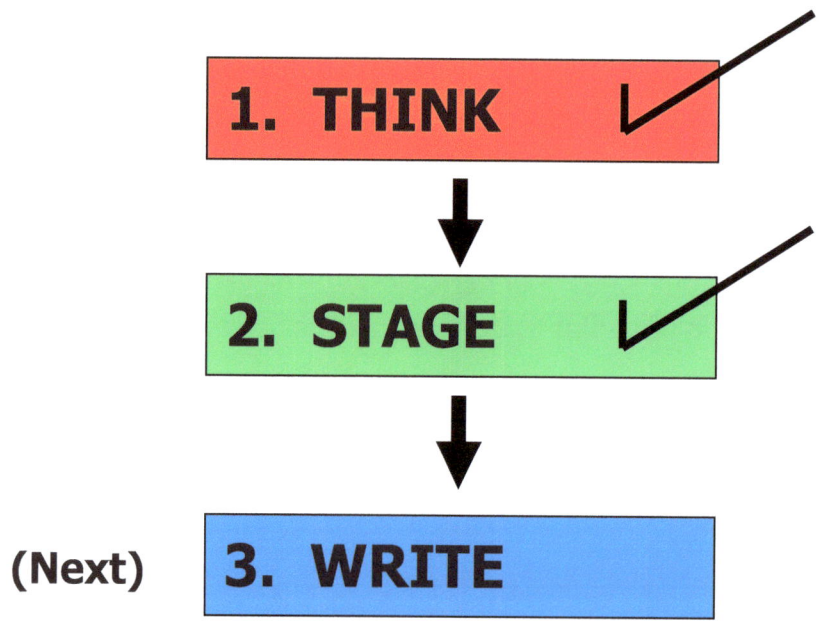

3. WRITE

> **3. WRITE:**
> 3-A. Use Three-Layer Model©
> 3-B. Engage Reader
> 3-C. Link Time to Clock

In this section, you will learn the secrets to:
- **Think clearly**
- **Write with style**
- **Write persuasive thoughts**
- **Finish on time**

Writing is the third step in our 3-step process. The Game Plan is THINK – STAGE – WRITE. Writing is the longest step in time, yet it is much longer and less productive for those who neglect to THINK and STAGE. Happily, you have completed these powerful steps and have positioned yourself to write a high scoring essay. You are at that moment in time, when you shift from Staging to Writing your essay.

Strategy Map for Writing Our Essay:

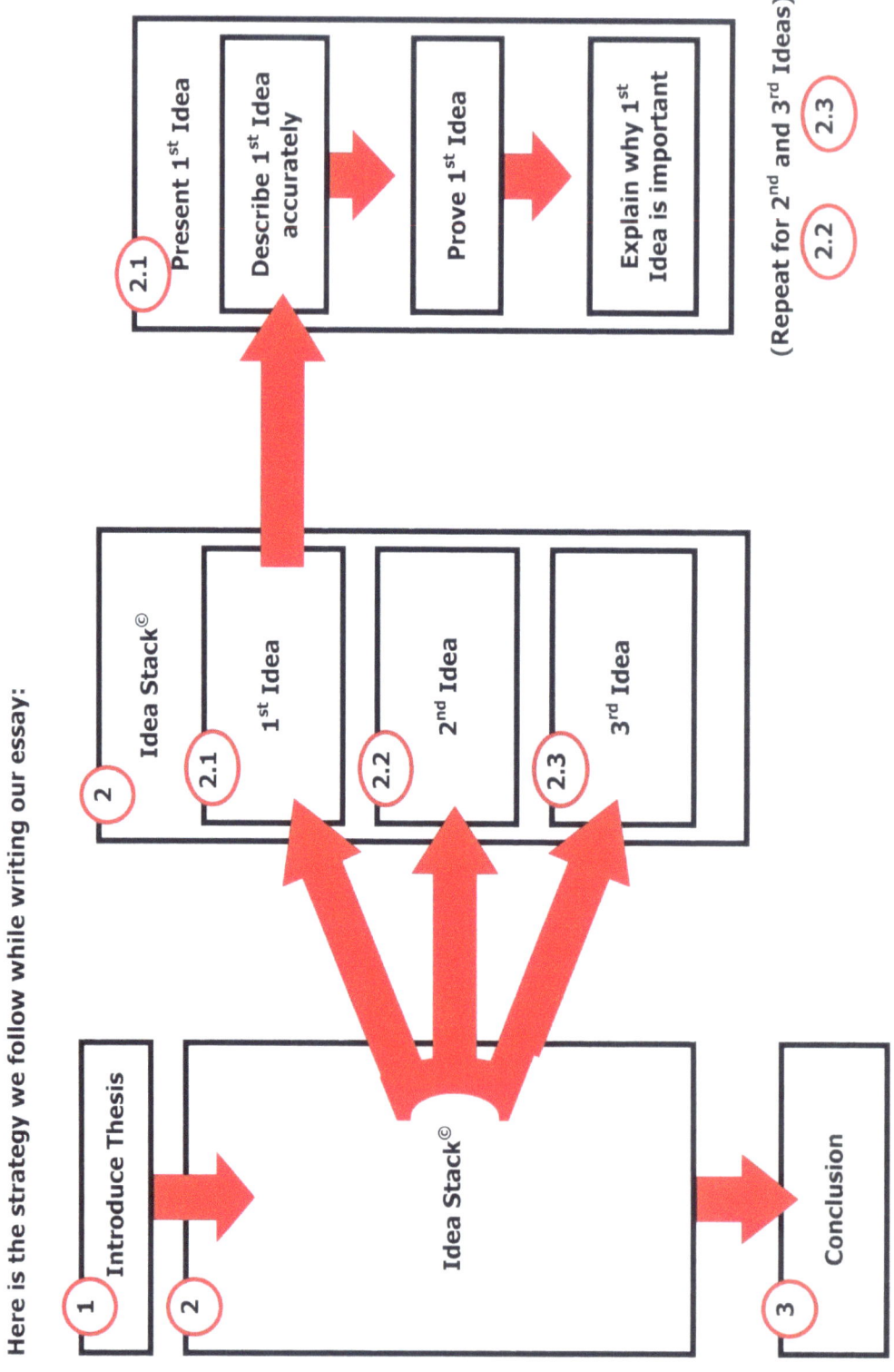

3-A. Writing Models

Models are a powerful way to grasp something that we have never thought before. The models that we are most familiar with are toys. A toy represents something bigger than itself. At the time of this writing, my daughter Madeline is twelve years old. We recently moved into a new home with a large bedroom where she could store her treasures. We added a curio cabinet with glass panels and a locking door to the furniture in her room. One day I noticed that Madeline had placed her treasures in there, everything from Cinderella's crystal slipper to china dolls and a mermaid snow globe. Much to my surprise, she also placed a plastic nested farm animal set inside the cabinet. The purple pig fits inside the blue sheep, which fits inside the brown cow. What made this plastic toy so special? It was the first toy that made her think. The plastic animals disappear as you stack them. As a toddler, they fascinated her. Our teachers know that a high scoring essay is one that puts ideas together one inside the other. The three-cup-stacking toy below is a visual model of how we present our ideas one inside the other.

The No-Study Solution! – Writing Essays

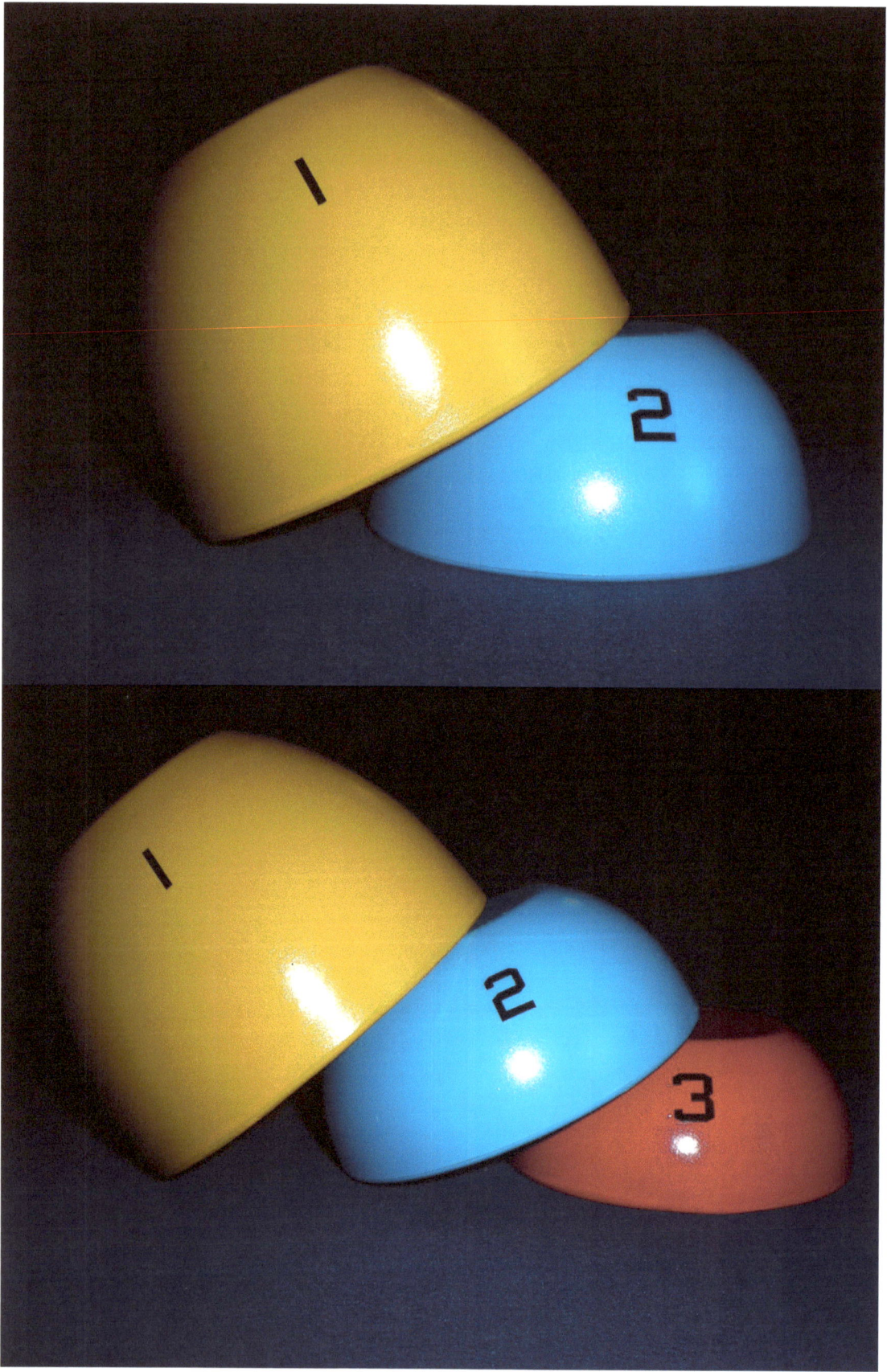

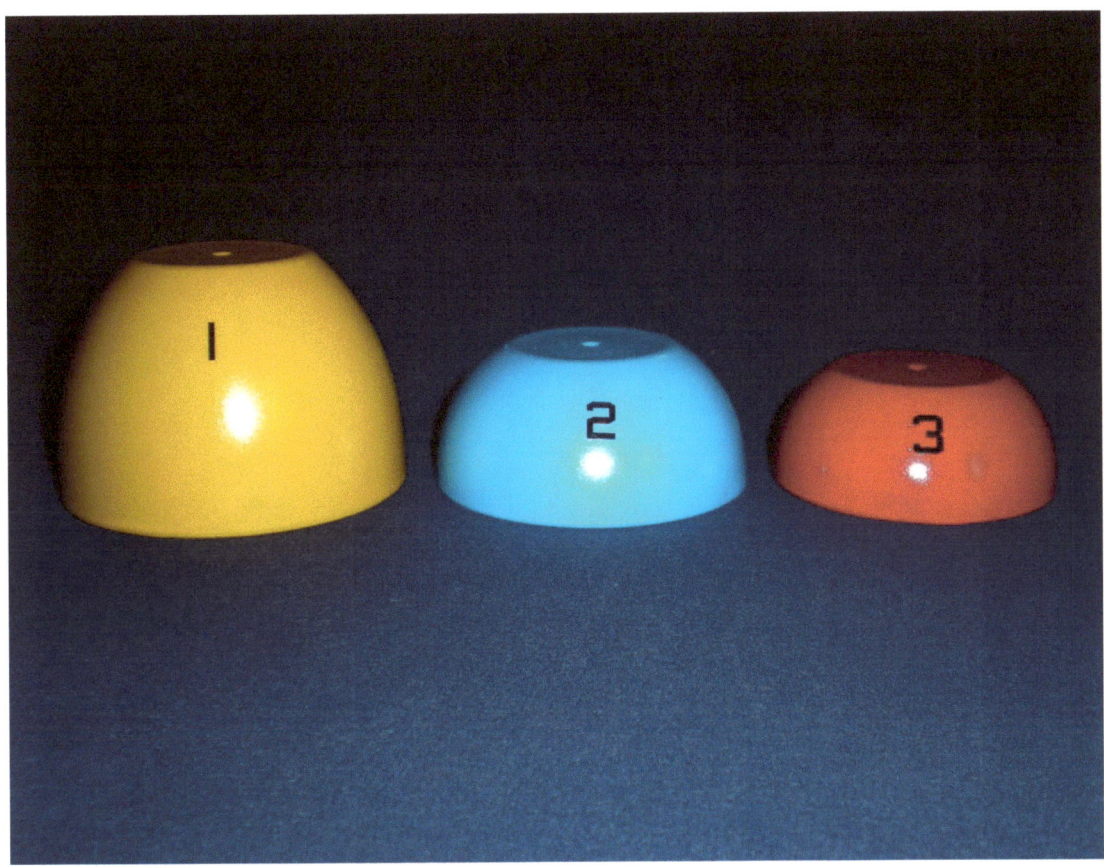

    The purpose of using a model, something that represents something else, is to shorten the time it takes to grasp a new concept – or in this case to write our essay. Understanding how the model works makes it so much easier to reproduce the real thing. Our goal while writing is to present our ideas in such a way as to fit the three structural layers in the same space – just as the Yellow, Blue and Red cups do in the photos on the previous pages.

    In this section we are modeling three structures that we use to present our Single-Thought Thesis© and Idea Stack©. In the photos on the preceding page, the Yellow, Blue and Red cups represent the three different structures. To use a real-life cooking analogy, imagine we are baking a cake. We could utilize all three of the cups to measure ingredients while making a cake or use just one. The use of one does not prevent the use of another – it just might take a few more scoops of a smaller cup. In the photo on the next page we see how one cup disappears inside the other, however, each cup's shape or size never changes. In the same way, we can write an essay using one, two or all three writing structures, and one does not rule out the use of another. Our models coexist beautifully. Our ideas, like ingredients, go in the cups.

It is valuable to gain a sense of the positive impact using a structure makes on an essay compared to following no design at all. Consider the impact of shape. Earning a high grade relies on how we shape our writing. Imagine the presentation of your next birthday cake. Forget about how old you will be, simply observe on the next page the two ways we can shape our cake – "A" and "B."

Cake A is shaped by cutting a rectangular piece of cake from the original cake. Cake B is shaped by cutting the same size piece of cake from the original cake and then squeezing the cake with our bare hands into a ball. Both pieces of cake contain the same ingredients. Both pieces started out the same size from the same cake. Both cakes use an identical attractive plate for presentation. However, which one would you rather eat?

Cake "A"

Cake "B"

    Similarly, when we write an essay, there is more to it than just presenting the right ideas. The shape and structure of our writing has a powerful influence on our grader, as powerful as the shaping above has on a cake's appeal. Cake presentation in the culinary arts typically occurs in manner "A," while essay writing in school usually occurs in manner "B."

Why does this happen? Because we do not think ahead to the finished product as we write. We have no clear model in our mind. Consider that the structuring of Cake A began by selecting a specific pan. A square pan produces a square cake while a round pan produces a round cake. The second part of cake making is the right ingredients. An angel cake made of egg whites is delicate and fluffy, while a pineapple upside down cake made of sugar, butter and pineapples is sweet and heavy. Translating this analogy to essay writing, the structural model we use is the pan and our ideas are the ingredients.

Writing an essay that earns us a higher grade begins with choosing the models (pans) we will use and then shaping our ideas (ingredients) to fit the pattern of those models. The best part about using models is that once we know them, we can use them repeatedly with little effort. The model describes the actual structure of the words in our written essay. Just as the cake looks like the pan from which it came, so will our essay read like the model we used to write it. There are three different "shapes" of our models. We now represent the models as boxes, which we will simply number one, two and three.

First, we will get to know each box individually. Then we will put them together and call the simultaneous use of all three, The Three-Layer Model©. These models stack just as the cups do, and since they are composed of written information, we will call them layers.

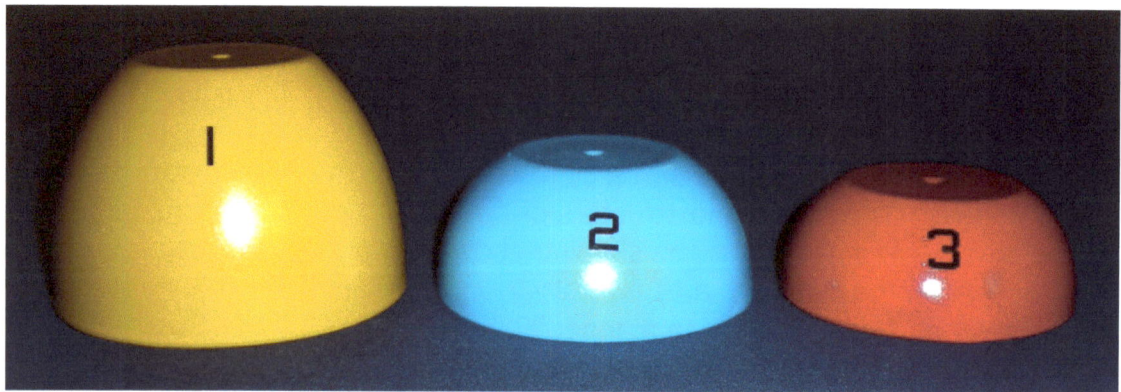

First Writing Model – The Design Layer

Key to the Three-Layer Writing Model©:
1 = The Design Layer
2 = The Idea Stack© Layer
3 = The Nail Down© Layer

Persuasive Communication by Design

We call the first layer **The Design**, because it works like a design or plan that when followed produces exactly what we intended – a sound essay. A design or plan leads to perfect follow through. Imagine, for example, a two-seat sports car. The car goes fast because the engineer designed it to do so. Imagine also, a pickup truck. The vehicle hauls a load of lumber because a different engineer designed it to do so. Neither vehicle can do the other's job. The raw materials, metal and electronics coming into the factory are for the most part, the same for both; however, the functionality of the vehicles rolling out the other end of the assembly line is quite different. While the sports car is fast and nimble, the pickup truck carries a lot of weight and is indestructible.

Rather than go fast or haul a big payload, we desire to achieve high grades. If we follow a design, one that describes a clear and convincing essay, that is exactly what we will write. So what precisely is this design? It tells a story with a beginning, middle and end. In the case of our essay, it is an introduction, presentation of ideas and conclusion. We use The Design Layer because this pattern increases the odds of convincing the reader of our thesis. Convincing people of something is so important to the world we live in, that businesses hire experts to do the convincing for them. These experts are salespeople. Salespeople convince others of a new point of view (think thesis).

My first career position after college was as a salesperson for IBM. The following story shows how powerful **The Design** is in real life communication, especially when combined with PERFORMANCE SECRET #3: Achieve common sense by being <u>curious</u> and asking questions about how something works. By using both, I was able to change the minds of seven men who were much older than I was; in fact, their combined business experience was 140 years greater than mine was.

My customer, Mr. Lofton, a Senior Vice President for the largest bank in Chicago comes to me saying, *"We have found a used computer that will save us some money, almost 50% at $1.4 million... and gives us more power than the new 4-engine computer you recommend. This gives us six-engines! Why don't you come by our staff meeting next Tuesday at 10 am and tell us if there is anything we should know before we buy this used computer."*

My first thought is to agree with my customer. Six engines sound more powerful than four engines. However, this means I will not have anything to say at the staff meeting on Tuesday. To figure out the truth about the computer's power, I start doing my research. I find out that the six used engines deliver a power of 77 and my four new engines deliver a power of 74. Not good! Regardless, my employer is paying me to convince them to THINK differently, to say, *"We want to buy a new computer from IBM, not a used IBM computer."* So, I turn to my one strategy that never fails – being curious and figuring out how something works. It is time to ask questions of the IBM System Engineers who are experts in the bank's software and ask them how it <u>really</u> works.

Of the 10,000 IBM employees in Chicago, only one is the best on this software. He stands out with his gray hair, silver beard and passionate swagger – a swagger that comes from a lifetime of doing what one loves. Everyone at IBM goes by his or her last name, except for him. He is simply Mr. Z.

> ***Mark:*** *Mr. Z, what do you know about how the bank's credit card authorization software works?*
>
> ***Mr. Z:*** *Oh, I know a lot about it.*
>
> ***Mark:*** *More than the people at the bank, who think it will run fine on a six-engine mainframe?*
>
> ***Mr. Z:*** *Of course.*
>
> ***Mark:*** *How is that?*
>
> ***Mr. Z:*** *They did not write the software... I did. I was the one who designed the software originally. I designed this credit card authorization software in the late 1960's [it is 1989] and I designed*

it to run as close to the machine code as possible. Now a days, the bank programmers just write extensions on top of what I did.

Mark: *Ok, so what does that mean to running across six engines?*

Mr. Z: *Well, the authorization software is hard coded to the address registers. Back in the 60's we only had one engine, so we could actually write to the commands in the engine. Your customer is going to have a problem, because even though most applications in their computer run on multiple engines at once, this one will not. This application performs all its calculations in one engine. If they are out of space on their current engine, the only option they have is to buy a new bigger engine from us. If not, they will hit a wall. The engine will keep spinning internally and get nothing done. Bank customers will not be able to charge their credit cards. We are the only computer manufacturer with the bigger engine. The used engines have a power of 12.8 and IBM's new engines have a power of 18.5. Our new engines are 45% faster!*

Mark: *Then, should I tell them that their CICS Application Region software can only run in one region because it references the storage registers in the machine code of their MVS-370 computer chip, consequently, they could not utilize more than one CPU in the IBM 3090-600E regardless of how many MIPS it could deliver?*

Mr. Z: *Well, not quite like that Mark. You have to tell them what you are going to tell them, tell them, and then tell them what you told them. You must <u>ease</u> into your message. You can't just come out and tell them everything at once. You are delivering information they have never heard before. The executives need time to absorb how the software works, so you will need to tell them three times.*

Mark: *Got it!*

Now it is Tuesday, and I am sitting in the conference room on one side of a very long mahogany table facing eight computer executives along the other side. Mr. Lofton starts the meeting and announces the first topic - what to do about the need for more power in their computer. Mr. Voss, the Vice President of Technology, shares his team's research that buying two more current model "E" engines for their four-engine computer will make it a more powerful six-engine mainframe and save the bank $1,400,000. The IBM proposal to spend more on new engines is a waste of money. As he finishes, Mr. Lofton says, *"Mark is there anything else we should know about this?"*

[**Introduction** -- Tell them what I am going to tell them]

"Well, gentlemen, although the six-engine mainframe you have found is a very nice computer, it won't work for your business. Your credit card software can only run on one engine. You need to find bigger engines, not more engines."

[**Idea Stack**© - Tell Them]

"Your business is validating all the credit card purchases of your customers on the biggest shopping day of the year, the day after Thanksgiving. To do that, you need to turn around the approval in 1.5 seconds, and that is going to take a faster engine than the E series you currently have and are looking to buy more of. Today you run four E engines on your IBM 3090-400E. Buying two more does not give you a faster engine. It just gives you more engines of the same speed. Your credit card authorization software was written in the early 1960's, when the IBM architecture only had one engine; your software was designed for speed, and that speed required hard coding to the address registers within the engine itself. Even though your operating system can multi-task, it cannot spread the load of the credit card authorization software across engines without re-writing it, which can take months, perhaps even years. Now the new model "S" engines I have proposed are 45% faster than the "E" engines, 18.5 MIPS compared to 12.8 MIPS. Yes, it costs more, $2,700,000, but it is the only viable option you have to get the job done – approving all the customer credit card transactions during Christmas shopping season. You grow every year, and last Christmas your computer hit 98% capacity on one engine. You will not make it through this season and keep your customers happy if you buy two more slow "E" engines."

[**Conclusion** - Tell Them What I Told Them]

"The good news, gentlemen, when you look at how your software actually works, is that the new "S" engine series will not only get you through this Christmas shopping season, but it will get you through one or two more seasons after that because the "S" series engine is 45% faster. While spending $1,400,000 for the two-used "E" engines provides no additional benefit, spending $2,700,000 does. This means customers will be happy as they shop, the bank will generate profits, and you can show the Chairman, Mr. Callaghan, that you made the low cost decision – an IBM "S" class Mainframe. Are there any questions? ...Thank you."

> **PERFORMANCE SECRET #15:** Explain your thesis three times:
> 1st - Tell them what you are going to tell them
> 2nd - Tell them
> 3rd - Tell them what you told them

This experience demonstrates three keys to success. First, always keep asking questions until you know how something works (Performance Secret #3). Second, use The Design to tell your story three times, each time with a different emphasis (Performance Secret #15). Third, just because someone knows more than you do, does not mean he will come to a better conclusion, (see we are already smart enough, page 9).

After our meeting, I made the sale and enjoyed the commission. Millions of Christmas shoppers charged up their credit cards on Black Friday. The shoppers got their gifts. The stores made their money. Each member of Mr. Lofton's executive team received an even larger year-end bonus than usual.

Everyone was happy.

Thank you, Mr. Z!

The Design Defined

Now we discover how **The Design** model works at a high level by looking at each of its three parts.

Introduction - The first time we tell our thesis to the reader our only objective is to present the idea – we do not want to explain it. We call this the Introduction.

Idea Stack© - The second time we tell them, we explain our thesis completely, that is we deliver the complete flow of thought supporting our position, including appropriate facts, details and implications – the Idea Stack©.

Conclusion - The third time we tell them, we are reinforcing the key ideas already presented with a summary – the Conclusion. Visually, we represent each part of the essay as a box, and label the boxes this way:

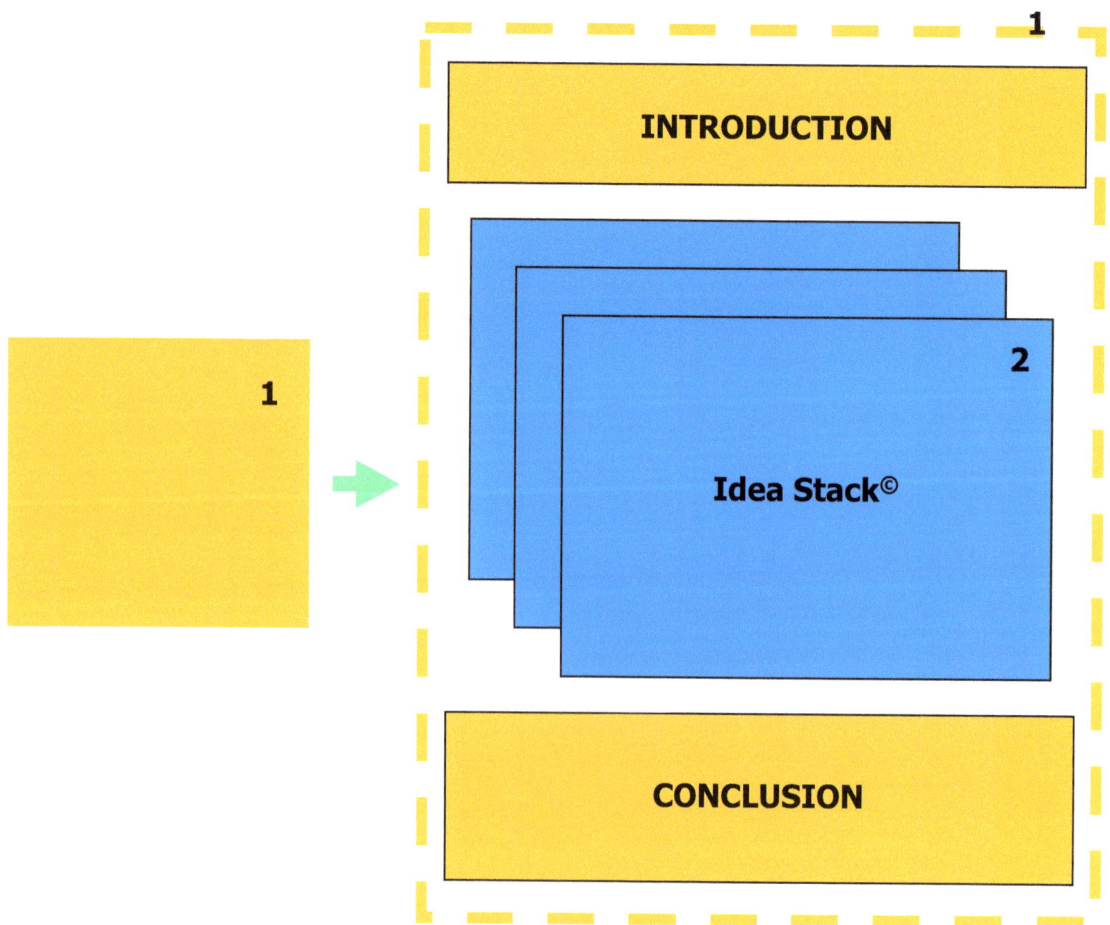

We illustrate this model as both a single box on the left, because it is one model or layer, and as three boxes on the right, because the model has three individual parts. This is practical because we can write or talk using The Design without being very good at the Idea Stack©. This means The Design can stand on its own. Likewise, the Idea Stack© (Tell Them) works on its own but is not nearly as effective without an Introduction and Conclusion. Happily, readers of this book will possess the tools to be good at all parts of The Design.

WRITING MODEL #1: The Design consists of an Introduction, an Idea Stack© and a Conclusion.

Writing the Introduction

Writing an Introduction is both science and art. Keeping the reader/grader interested requires both structure and emotion. I developed a strategy that makes delivering both... easy. It is named **"HIT© - How to Put Style into the Introduction"** on pages 135-138. Rather than discuss the Introduction twice, I chose to present how to write an Introduction later when we talk about how to keep the reader/grader awake. This section is called "Engaging the Reader" which starts on page 134. Feel free to go ahead and read about how to write an Introduction. After that, remember to come back here.

For those of you who are moving along with our current conversation, let's assume that we <u>have</u> written the Introduction, and we are now moving on to that Blue cup, The Second Writing Model – the Idea Stack©. Although we are familiar with the stack itself, we have not yet covered effective strategies for writing from it. Since we told the reader/grader, what we are <u>going</u> <u>to</u> <u>tell</u> <u>them</u> with the Introduction, now it is important to <u>tell</u> <u>them</u>.

Second Writing Model – The Idea Stack© Layer

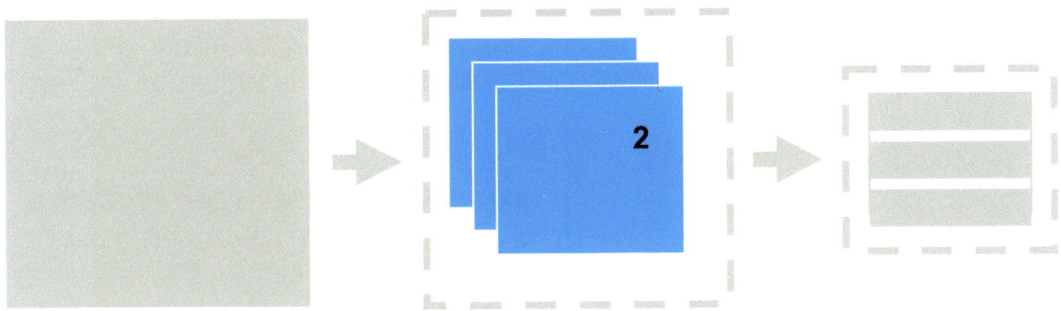

Key to the Three-Layer Writing Model©:
    1 = The Design Layer
    2 = The Idea Stack© Layer
    3 = The Nail Down© Layer

Writing from an Idea Stack©

We talked about writing from an Idea Stack© for some time and now we will illustrate exactly how to do this. The simplest way to present our thesis is to write our essay on the right by following the numbers in the outline on the left:

DOGS BEST
_____

2 – WORK
4 – SIGHT DOGS
3 – POLICE K-9
8 – BITE THIEVES
5 – RACING
9 – PLAY CATCH
6 – PROTECT FAMILY
~~– LIVE 10-14 YEARS~~
10 – HANG OUT
~~– WALK 2 X A DAY~~
1 – TRAINABLE
7 – BARK LOUD

Dogs deliver superior value to society over cats because people can train[1] them to follow spoken commands.

Compared to cats, dogs possess the unique ability to follow words spoken by humans. Dogs have performed work[2] such as sheep herding since ancient times. Dogs perform Police[3] work today throughout airports and cities of America. They do whatever trained commands their handlers give them. Sight dogs[4] are trained by experts through speech and touch, and then given to the blind as their daily guides and companions. The dogs' ability to be trained to perform complex tasks is what makes them so valuable. Some value may be questionable, such the entertainment of racing[5], never the less, while doing so, dogs demonstrate their ability to be trained to perform with exactness. Dogs deliver priceless safety to people simply by being in a family[6] home, barking[7], and having a reputation to bite[8] intruders. Perhaps the greatest value dogs provide is the companionship of playing catch[9], hanging out[10] and going on walks.

As has been shown above, dogs provide valuable services to both pet owners and society as a whole due to their ability to learn and follow spoken commands. The result is that both society and pet owners are better off with these valuable services performed, services that cats cannot provide.

Fast Food

The essay on the previous page is an offensive minded essay, using only the Thinking strategies and tools of section "1-A Think up the Ideas". The essay does not take into account the defensive strategies and tools of sections "1-B How to De-BUGS© the Ideas" and "1-C Defuse Counter-Ideas". Therefore, I left in idea #5 – *Racing*. When an essay is exclusively offensive in nature, it leaves the other point of view alone. If this basic approach works for you, especially, first time readers, feel free to write your essays from this one-dimensional mindset. For those of you ready to run a balanced approach, we are now going to look at marketing techniques used by the fast food industry. While the fast food industry entices us to spend more money on their products, with dubious health effects, we simply will use the psychology behind their marketing to improve the scores on our essays.

Consider the choices we get to make when looking at a fast food menu, perhaps even through the vantage point of our car window. For many food types, such as hamburgers, fries and drinks, restaurants present different sizes of essentially the same product: a single or double cheeseburger or double bacon cheeseburger for a sandwich, the same beverages dispensed in different size cups or collectable glasses. Even salads appear on the 99-cent menu and again on a full course menu. Regardless of what we like to eat, there is a subconscious pattern guiding our decision-making. The presentation of choices is usually in a pattern of three options: Small, Medium and Large.

When restaurants present us three options, they play on the human tendency to want to be in control and the desire to feel we are making the smart choice. In order for this to happen, we must have options. When we have three options, we feel as though we are choosing from a complete set of research. Three is an easy number to choose from conceptually. People are short, average or tall. Cars are either compact, mid-size or luxury. If we have one of each class to choose from, on a subconscious level, we are making an informed choice.

How do the three choices satisfy the subconscious? When we see things from one location, we view everything beyond where we are as either closer or farther away. Objects are smaller than we are or bigger than we are. Situations are worse or better. Things are slower or faster. People are rude or friendly. Potential activities appear as either boring or exciting. The number three encompasses all choices on a subconscious level from our vantage point.

What does this mean for the person grading our essay? She will experience our proof as complete on a subconscious level when we present three ideas in support of a thesis. This happens because she will view two of our ideas as either smaller or bigger than our first idea. In the behavior of making choices, we will have provided all that is required to make a correct choice – three options.

Obviously, we must provide the teacher with relevant and accurate facts to back our idea; however, we will never worry if we have done enough. Now we know that once we have presented three examples, our teacher's subconscious and emotional grading system will judge our presentation complete. Keep in mind that on a logical or analytical level, the test question may require <u>more</u> ideas to <u>prove</u> a concept <u>completely</u>; however, our strategy is <u>never</u> to <u>present</u> <u>less</u> than <u>three</u> ideas. Whenever we are short, we simply manufacture one or two more ideas until we have three. With this strategy in mind, the Second Writing Model – the Idea Stack© Layer consists of three ideas:

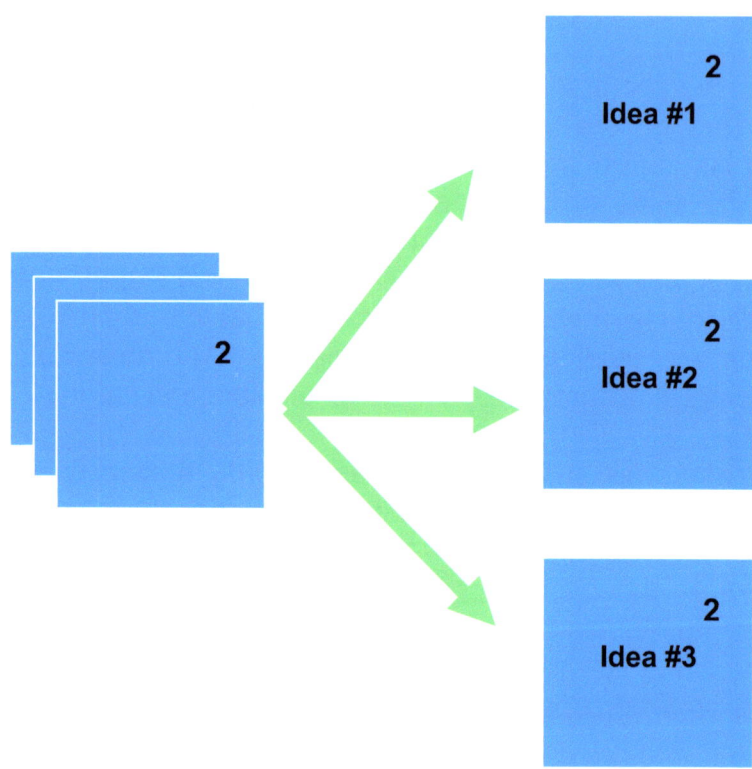

PERFORMANCE SECRET #16: Present three ideas in support of your thesis in order to satisfy the grader's subconscious checklist.

All Ideas Are Not Created Equal

Although Thomas Jefferson was on to a profound truth when he wrote, "all <u>men</u> are created equal" in the Declaration of Independence, we cannot extend that concept to all <u>things</u> being created equal – especially if those things are the ideas we present in our essay. Up until now, in **Dogs vs. Cats,** we have assumed that all the ideas are of equal value and numbered them 1-10. However, it is obvious that each idea delivers proof at a different level of persuasive strength. So, how do we sequence our ideas to write the most persuasive essay? We strengthen individual ideas by bundling them. We notice which ones are related, and place them in groups, like this:

Work	Bite Intruders	Play Catch
Sight Dogs	Protect Family	Hang Out
Police K-9's	Bark Loud	
Trainable		

Now we look through each bundle to find the word that is the theme for all the ideas in that box. After some thinking, we come up with the following:

Trainable	**Protectors**	**Companionship**

Trainable is both an idea and the common thread of the ideas in the first box. In the second box we key in on the word "protect," realizing that it defines the role dogs play as they bite robbers, bark and keep the family safe. For the third group, we do not see an idea itself as a common thread or key. Therefore, we choose to invent a common theme for this box, and that is **Companionship**. The remaining ideas support each theme, so we place the ideas back under their respective themes to generate the following lists:

Trainable	**Protectors**	**Companionship**
Work	Bark Loud	Hang Out
Police K-9's	Bite Intruders	Play Catch
Sight Dogs		

Looking at our T-View Outline©, we recall a nice defuse for the extra care dogs require, such as deploying rat poison to offset a cat's protective value of hunting rats. (Review The Replacement Approach© on pages 68-70).

Trainable	**Protectors**	**Companionship**
Work	Bark Loud	Hang Out
Police K-9's	Bite Intruders	Play Catch
Sight Dogs	Rat Poison (defuse)	

Plugging our bundles into the Second Writing Model – The Idea Stack©, we arrive at a stack of three main ideas where each is supported by lesser ideas:

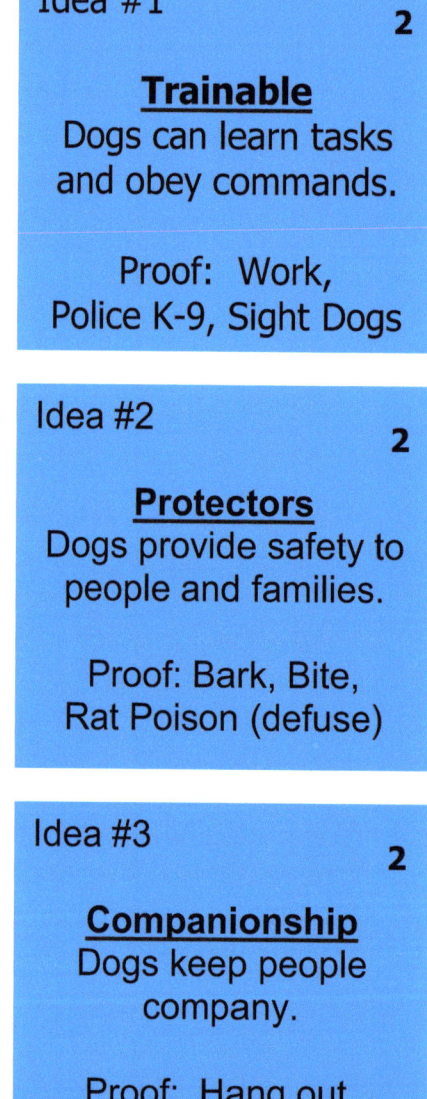

Our Idea Stack© is complete. We identified three ideas that prove dogs provide higher social value. Now it is time for us to WRITE our first idea.

> **WRITING MODEL #2:** The Idea Stack© lists all the ideas and **numbers them in the most convincing order.**

Third Writing Model – The Nail Down© Layer

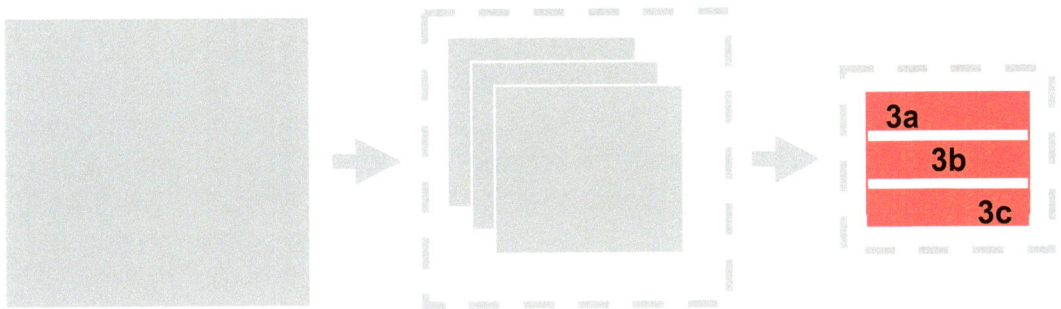

Key to the Three-Layer Writing Model©:
    1 = The Design Layer
    2 = The Idea Stack© Layer
    3 = The Nail Down© Layer

1

2

3

4

The Nail Down©

How do we write each idea? We'll start with an analogy. Have you ever picked up a hammer, held a nail between two fingers and started to drive the nail into a piece of wood? The nail slides a short distance with each strike of the hammer. There is a sharp ping when metal collides with metal. The further you drive the nail down into the wood, the steadier it becomes. Soon you no longer hold the nail, and with a final swing or two, you drive the nail down into the wood. The nail will go no farther. The head of the nail is below the surface of the wood. Once the nail's head is imbedded this deeply, the nail becomes impossible to pull out without damaging the wood. One could say, *"That nail's never coming out."*

The **Nail Down**© is a writing strategy that makes an unforgettable impression on our reader. Imagine if our words go into his brain as deeply as our nail did into the wood – it would make a lasting impression. To achieve this level of persuasion we write three sentences, one sentence each that:
- **D**escribes our idea
- **P**roves our idea
- Tells why our idea is **I**mportant

In actuality, we may write more than one sentence to cover each of the three steps of the Nail Down©, however we need at least one sentence of each step. Given the crucial nature of needing all three parts, we create a performance rule for ourselves that says:

> **Always break the Nail Down© into at least three sentences, one of each type.**

Now we have a fail-safe mechanism in our game to assure that we don't miss one of these key components. For those of us who like acronyms, we use **DPI** to remember: **D**escribe, **P**rove and **I**mportant.

WRITING MODEL #3: The Nail Down© writes each idea by **D**escribing it, **P**roving it and telling why it is **I**mportant.

Next, we will discuss how to write each part of **DPI** effectively.

Describe Our Idea

We get our bearings by remembering PERFORMANCE SECRET #15 – Explain your thesis three times. Then, realizing that because we have already told them what we were going to tell them in the Introduction, we are now in the second telling of the thesis – the "tell them" part. Here our primary goal is to be accurate. Accuracy communicates to the grader that we know the class material and that perception improves our score. In **Dogs vs. Cats**, our first idea is that dogs are trainable. It is important for us to describe exactly what we mean by that, so we use the **D**escribe step of this writing model to write exactly what we mean by trainable:

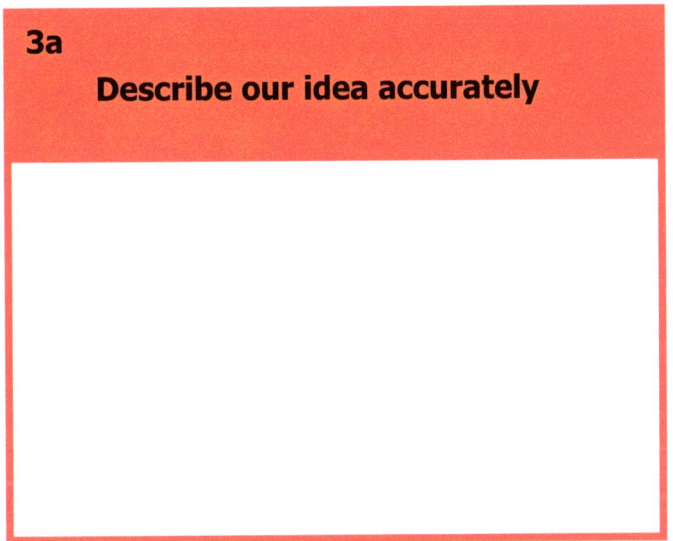

Among domesticated animals, dogs uniquely possess the ability to be trained to follow spoken commands. We find people training dogs commercially and privately. Commercially, police dogs are trained as puppies to follow the commands: sit, down, stay, heel and come here. Later, as adults, these dogs are trained to attack criminals and retreat, sniff out weapons and drugs, and detain suspects. Privately, dog owners train their personal pets to walk on a leash, sit, stay, come, hunt, play fetch, catch the flying disc, ride skateboards, jump on snowboards, and retrieve newspapers. These activities prove that dogs can be trained to follow spoken commands.

We now feel confident knowing that we have completed the first step in the Nail Down©. We have driven the nail in far enough that it stands up on its own. We have completely described our idea that "Dogs possess the ability to be trained to perform specific tasks." Next, we will start driving the nail deeper into the wood with strong powerful swings of the hammer. We will use proof to support our description.

Prove Our Idea

We now continue with the Nail Down© by glancing at our Idea Stack© looking for any facts, detail or information that **P**roves or supports the main idea we just described – "Trainable". We will continue following our model by presenting a supporting detail "Police K-9":

> **3b**
> **Prove our idea with facts, detail, logic or analysis.**

Police work is a valuable benefit that dogs provide to society today. Despite the highly advanced state of technology, Police dogs still provide services unmatched by any other source. While performing police fieldwork, a K-9 German Shepherd can sense the direction of a fleeing suspect beyond the range of portable infrared devices. Additionally, dogs can detect the presence of suspects invisible to the human eye. Once apprehended, the police dog will attack or stand down on command. The dog will also watch the suspect as the officer approaches and will warn or respond as necessary should the suspect attempt to flee or draw a weapon. Police dogs generate more fear in most people than a second officer does. I observed this personally in a ride-along with a K-9 team. Police dogs are the most cost-effective and pervasive detector of explosive devices and illegal drugs in airport security today. Overseas, the US military has deployed 70 dogs in Afghanistan with plans to increase their numbers to 219 in July 2010. In one month, these dogs discovered 20 unexploded bombs, saving the lives of our troops.

We have now provided sufficient details to prove that dogs deliver more value to society because they can follow spoken commands. We showed how dogs work alongside humans in what is probably the most demanding workplace on earth – military combat. This is impressive proof. We have driven the nail down to within one strike of imbedding its head below the surface of the wood.

Tell Why It is Important

We will now complete our Nail Down©, and drive the nail below the surface of the wood by stating <u>why</u> the idea is **I**mportant. Recall that our example essay question asks us **"Which pet generates the most value to both the pet owner and society as a whole?"** Wouldn't it make sense to tell our reader <u>why</u> we said what we said? The answer is absolutely – Yes! Especially, when we consider the reason why we are answering an essay question in the first place. The essay question goes beyond a mere fill-in-the-blank or multiple-choice question and forces us to explain <u>why</u> we gave the answer we gave. How do we know this? Human beings follow the path of least resistance, and it would be much easier for the teacher to create a test of multiple choice or fill in the blank questions. So just by getting the essay type question, we know that this third part of the Nail Down© is where we earn the extra grade points. It is when we tell the reader/grader one of the following:

- <u>Why</u> the idea is **I**mportant
- <u>What</u> <u>this</u> idea <u>means</u>
- The <u>significance</u> of our proof
- The <u>implication</u> of our idea

In ***Dogs vs. Cats***, we write the **I**mportance this way:

The security work police dogs perform is significant for two reasons. First, they often perform jobs humans cannot perform. Humans cannot follow the trail of a missing person the way a Bloodhound can. Second, they can take on tasks too dangerous for humans. War dogs can identify hidden bombs that humans cannot see, thereby preserving soldiers' lives. All these security benefits at home and abroad are made possible by a dog's ability to be trained by human communication. In today's financially challenged environment, it is vital to utilize low cost and effective solutions such as these police and military dogs to maximize the public good.

In this paragraph, we have stated exactly <u>why</u> this idea is <u>important</u>. What is more significant than saving lives and saving money? Who would want to challenge this argument? We can rest peacefully knowing we have made a convincing point.

Telling our grader why the information we presented is important places our essay writing on an advanced level. For example, a brilliant graduate student wrote Essay IV, **The Future of Science**, pages 183-185. Notice that he does not even bring up an idea, without telling why it is important. For example:

Leeuwenhoek, in the 1600s, discovered cells through the manipulation of an optical microscope. He used the best instruments available in his time, and he learned a great deal about the nature of life. However, <u>the</u> <u>information</u> he collected <u>was limited</u>.

As college students, we are often baffled when taking upper division classes for the first time. These 300 and 400 level courses (or 3rd and 4th year classes) demand from us the <u>Why</u> **I**mportant piece of the Nail Down©. This level of critical thinking is what defines these courses. Now that you know this, you will not be surprised when you get there!

When we neglect to tell the reader/grader what we believe is "stating the obvious," we rob the grader of seeing how <u>deeply</u> <u>we</u> <u>think</u>. She cannot find out about <u>our</u> <u>unique</u> <u>insights</u> nor assess <u>how</u> <u>much</u> we learned in her class. Our job on the essay test is to show what thinking we have done and to link our thinking to meaningful conclusions. Remembering to tell why an idea is **I**mportant completes our communication.

Here are some other creative words we can use to keep our Nail Down© fresh when telling <u>why</u> an idea is **I**mportant:
- ramification
- implication
- result
- benefit

The Nail Down© is the way we prove each idea. We use the Nail Down© to convince the reader/grader that our idea is important by leading her through a path of thought that is both logical proof and emotional proof. This writing model gives us the ability to influence her perception of our writing. Consider for a moment, that most scientists will agree that human beings are both right brained and left brained creatures. To maximize our grade, we must address both sides of the human decision system. Proving our idea through a **DP** (Describe, Prove) convinces the left side of the brain that our idea is logical, true or valid. Proving our idea through an **I** (Important) convinces the right side of the brain that this idea is worthy, valuable or vital. We have arrived back at our acronym **DPI**, which is where we started our conversation of the Nail Down©.

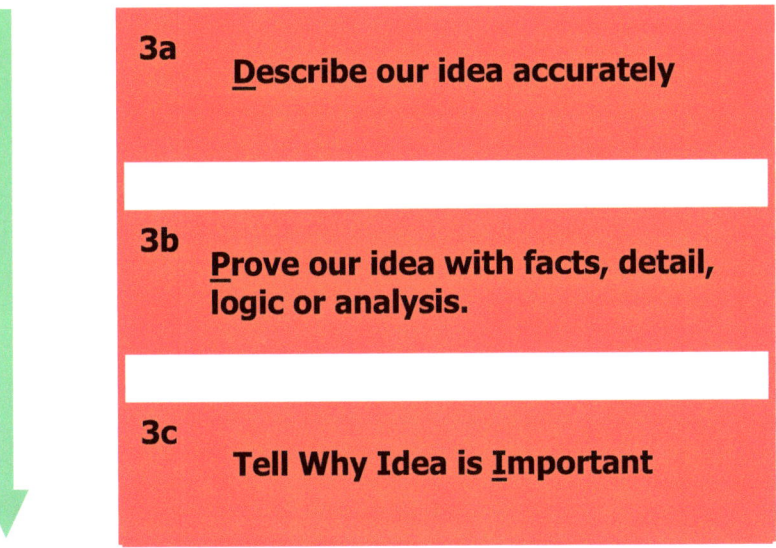

Writing with the intent to convince both the logical and emotional person frees us up from worry about what our teacher wants. Every grader is going to be one or the other or a mixture. This knowledge alone should reduce our level of test anxiety. From a teacher's perspective, great writing is not just about <u>what</u> we say, but <u>how</u> <u>well</u> we say it. The Nail Down© is a tool that achieves both.

PERFORMANCE SECRET #17: Tell the reader why each idea is important. Do not leave it up to the reader to figure out.

The Three-Layer Model© is Complete

Each of you picked up this book for a reason. Your specific reasons will vary, however most will fall in the area of *"Looking for ways to get higher grades."* The three-layer nature of our writing models makes them easy to learn and simple to use. Learning any one layer will improve your writing. Learning them all will allow you to earn the best grade you can possibly achieve.

Imagine being the master of all three models. You always know where you are and what you have left to write. You never have to stop, think, regroup and hope to get back on track. You have your plan and you are having fun executing your plan. Your attitude is *"Let's roll"* instead of anticipating the *"Agony of defeat."* You are writing instinctively. Your thoughts flow onto paper or keyboard effortlessly. You use each model separately, in pairs or simultaneously as the situation dictates. You are able to convince the teacher that your thoughts are original and valid. While you write, you have the satisfaction of knowing you are going to score a high grade. To achieve all these benefits, I invite you master the Three-Layer Model©.

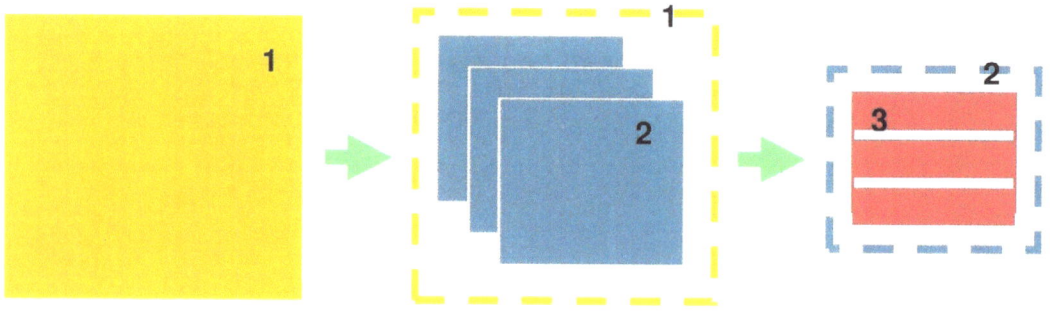

STRATEGY TOOL #7: Use all Three Layers simultaneously to achieve a persuasive argument that proves your thesis.

When to Write What Guide©

Here is a view of The Three-Layer Model© that answers the question — what do I write and when do I write it? The grid below shows the location within our essay to place different types of information. The type of information shows across the top of the grid and the location is along the side of the grid:

	CONCEPTS	FACTS, DETAIL AND INFORMATION	WHY IMPORTANT
INTRODUCTION	**Yes,** Thesis	**No**	**No**
IDEA STACK©	**Yes,** Idea 1 / Idea 2 / Idea 3	**Yes,** Proof for Idea 1 / Proof for Idea 2 / Proof for Idea 3	**Yes,** Why Idea 1 Important / Why Idea 2 Important / Why Idea 3 Important
CONCLUSION	**Yes,** Restate Thesis	**Brief,** Short Review of the Key Findings that Prove your Thesis	**Yes,** What the Thesis means now that you proved it

> **STRATEGY TOOL #8:** Use the When to Write What Guide© to select the type of information to place within each section of the essay.

The No-Study Solution! – Writing Essays

3-B. Engage the Reader

Intuitively we know, on some level, that our essay's grade really depends upon how "good" of a writer we are. Since many of us believe that good writers are born, not made, we tend to give up hope. In this section, we will debunk this myth by showing how good writers write and break their techniques down into easy-to-follow steps. Soon you will be able to emulate their skills and grab the reader's attention. I invite you to be open to the possibility that "good" writing may be easier than you think.

Like many skills, good writing follows patterns. Authors often write in their own rhythm. Thus, we can identify an author's technique. By imitating the author's patterns, the everyday student can achieve a high level of performance. We will start by noticing that there is a difference between organization and style. Organization is the skill of placing ideas and information in the best location to support a persuasive argument and achieve the highest grade. Until now, this has been our primary focus. We are shifting our focus to address style, because <u>someone</u> actually <u>has</u> to <u>read</u> our <u>writing</u>. The more appealing it is to our grader, the more likely we are to receive a pleasing grade.

Let's introduce style by talking about the reader experience. Most of us can accept the idea that music creates a mood or feeling in the ear of the listener. Taking this insight and relating it to writing, the closer we match the feel of our information to the subject of our information, the more successful we will be. Just as surfer music works better in a teen beach movie than in a crime drama, matching the feel of our writing to our subject not only grabs the reader's attention, it also makes our presentation more powerful than mere facts and logic. One way to bring feel to our writing is to imagine the personality of the reader. What will he experience while reading our essay? We imagine (1) what the reader will see, (2) how he will feel while reading it and (3) what he will hear in his mind as he follows our conversation. In Essay V, **New Airport in Chicago**, starting on page 187, the student used this Performance Secret to adapt his normal writing to the visual style of a business publication, the sound of a confident communicator and the feel of a consultant making a recommendation. Matching the <u>sight</u>, <u>sound</u> and <u>feel</u> of our writing to our target reader's personality is the beginning of writing in an engaging style.

PERFORMANCE SECRET #18: Relate to the reader on an emotional level. Consider what he will <u>see, hear</u> and <u>feel</u>. Write in a manner and mood that the appeals to the reader.

HIT© - How to Put Style into the Introduction

It is time to write our introduction. Now that we understand what goes into an introduction and what comes after it, we are ready to write the most powerful and engaging introduction humanly possible.

Specifically, we are going to design the introduction so that it grabs our reader/grader's attention and presents a clear thesis – and nothing else. We must achieve three objectives to do this: **(1)** pique her interest, **(2)** appear credible and **(3)** state our thesis. When our grader finishes reading our introduction, she will be thinking, *"This could be an "A."*

Recall that we are simply telling them <u>what</u> we are going to tell them. We are not going to tell it. The telling of the story is the mission of the Idea Stack©. By keeping the ideas out of the introduction, we maintain momentum with our reader. We pull her into the heart of our essay. This is important since our grader will be reading many essays on the same topic in a short timeframe. Brevity is one secret to writing an engaging introduction. Best-selling authors often start their books with crisp short sentences.

We start by imagining our introduction as three sentences, one matched to achieve each objective. Use the acronym **HIT©** to remember the strategy.
- **(1) H**ello Sentence
- **(2) I**ssue/Key Principle Sentence
- **(3) T**hesis Sentence

(1) Hello Sentence – The objective here is to get the reader warmed up and to catch her interest. Unlike the reading of published books, magazines and newspapers, our reader is going to experience multiple essays on the identical subject. Being like everyone else is not going to work. Luckily, there are many well-written examples of **H**ello Sentences available. Where do we find them? We look at the first paragraphs in newspaper articles, magazine articles, scientific journals and books. Why not go for the best and analyze the opening sentence of an award winning writer or best-selling author? As we examine how each author opens to his audience, we see that he uses a pattern or device. Even the finest writers are predictable and repetitive with their art. Then we imitate that device and blend our own style with it. I will share three devices I discovered through such examination:

- **Connect to the Human Experience** – The idea is to draw in the reader by causing her to connect emotionally with a familiar experience in life. Every human being wants to feel as though others understand her. Bringing in an everyday annoyance, challenge or task to which the reader can relate is one way to make that connection. We can find these experiences by observing what people do each day and how they react emotionally to the events around them. In Essay V, **New Airport in Chicago**, page 187, the student starts with a human experience most business people can relate to – making a difficult choice. In fact, almost anybody breathing today can relate to facing difficult choices, as they are simply part of life. There is much emotion loaded into making big decisions. The essay begins *"Mayor Daley is faced with a tough decision given three choices."* Actually, it is not Mayor Daley making the tough decision at all, but rather the student answering the essay question, an irony we are sure the teacher appreciated. This clever irony kept the grader awake if for no other reason than to see what other interesting comments the student would make.

- **Cut to the Action** – The objective is to place a visual picture of a dramatic scene in our reader's mind or an emotion in their heart to start our essay. In Essay III, **Risk**, page 180, the student's first sentence paints a picture: *"Inside Las Vegas casinos, a human drama is enacted as people win fortunes and lose paychecks."* Most Americans, even those who have not been to Las Vegas, can easily relate to this casino scene having watched one on TV or in the movies. Even without that, most Americans can relate to a paycheck, and the idea of losing an entire week's pay is certain to trigger an emotion within the heart of the reader.

- **Clever-Thought-Twist**© – The objective is to mention something interesting we know, not related to our topic, which heightens the interest of our topic through the association with that something we know. We are building a comparative insight. In Essay I, **What Rome Could Teach Romeo and Juliet**, page 172, the student used her fascination with Roman Architecture to start out her essay on Shakespeare. *"A keystone is the rock that fits in the top of an arch and holds it together. It was invented by the Romans to hold their aqueducts together, without it the arches would have crashed to the ground. Honesty is a keystone character trait that holds people's lives together."* **Roll Over, Fluffy!**, page 157, begins with *"A cursory look at Ancient Egyptian art reveals that dogs participated at the forefront of their military and leadership activities, yet today, nearly 5,000 years later, the question of whether a dog or a cat delivers the most value still lingers in some people's minds."* The thought twist is that – if the Egyptians figured this out 5,000 years ago, why didn't my teacher figure this out now?

PERFORMANCE SECRET #19: Grab the reader's attention by connecting to the human experience, cutting to the action and using Clever-Thought-Twists©.

---

(2) Issue/Key Principle Sentence – The objective here is to signal to the grader that we know what this question is looking for. If the teacher realizes that we are on to the key principle around the question, he will look favorably on our response from the beginning. We have already generated our own credibility! By using this sentence, we show that we have listened in class, that we understand the most important aspects of the course, and that as a result, our answer will be credible! What better way to start an essay than by convincing the grader that we already we know what we are talking about?

- **Reveal Key Issue** – We find Key Issues in essay questions about cultural, societal and political subjects. The key issue of ***Dogs vs. Cats*** is the benefit of owning the pet you like. In **Roll Over, Fluffy!** (the "Dog is Better") essay, the key issue is revealed: *"Dogs possess the ability to … perform specific and complex tasks … that improve people's lives."* Meanwhile, in **Cats Rule, Dogs Drool** (the "Cat is Better" essay), *"For companionship, health, and ease, the cat is the most obvious choice."* Each student has called out the key issue. With Dogs, the issue is what a dog can do, while with Cats the issue is quality of life for the pet owner.

- **Reveal Key Principle** – We find Key Principles in essay questions about math, science and economics. The second sentence in **New Airport in Chicago** is a Key Principle Sentence. The student shows the teacher that he understands how the most important economic principles in the course work together. *"There is competition among the airports for traffic and freight, so the airport must be put in a location where Demand can support an airport operating at the lowest point on its Survival Curve."* The student gains credibility on sentence two when the teacher realizes the student knows the driving principle within the essay question. Rather than force our grader to struggle figuring out what we know about the principles related to the essay question, why not just come out and tell them that we do? Use of this sentence greatly enhances our chances of earning an A.

(3) Our Thesis Sentence – The objective of our thesis sentence is to tell the reader what we are going to prove or what insight we will deliver. We have already discussed how to create the thesis in Staging on pages 79-83. Now we can see the wisdom of creating a thesis statement that we can write in a single thought. Under the **HIT**© strategy, we use a one-sentence thesis. A single thought will not take more than one-sentence. Simply insert your Single-Thought Thesis© in the third sentence slot of your introduction – and you are done!

Consider this. Anybody will listen to just about anything for 15 seconds, and 15 seconds is about the most time it would take anybody to read three sentences. The three-sentence design of the **HIT**© strategy meets both 15 second assumptions. To read an example of a **HIT**© strategy written under the real-world constraints of a timed exam, see **New Airport in Chicago**, page 187.

After we grab the grader's attention, we always **HIT**© them with the Key Principle and the Single-Thought Thesis© because when we do, the grader knows that we are going to focus on the answer they seek. By delivering these sentences, we are announcing to them ahead of time that we have nailed the question. For a real-life example, I have reproduced the original hand written test page from **New Airport in Chicago** on page 148. The alert reader will observe that my grader checked off the thesis sentence beside the words *"operating at the lowest point on its survival curve."* He saw that my thesis was correct and based upon the Key Principle the question was built to test. This red check is in-class positive proof that the **HIT**© strategy improves scores.

STRATEGY TOOL #9: Use the HIT© approach to write an engaging and credible Introduction.
- **H**ello Sentence
- **I**ssue / Key Principle Sentence
- **T**hesis Sentence

Title Strategies

The first words our grader will read in most essays is the title. How much thought do we put into these words? The simple way to write a catchy title is to wait until after we have written our essay. Now with the finished product before us, we can use it to inspire a Clever-Thought-Twist©. The following examples illustrate this creative art and the thought process behind each title:

I. **What Ancient Rome Could Teach Romeo and Juliet** (page 172) - The student presented the concept of a keystone shaped rock being the critical piece that enabled the arch to support a tremendous weight. This set up a parallel for the impact honesty has in one's character makeup. She took the Clever-Thought-Twist© of the keystone one-step farther. The title suggests that Romeo and Juliet had Roman architecture available in their day to observe. Had they looked at it and applied the concept of a single stone delivering structural integrity, would they have looked at their own lives and drawn a corollary? Given their impetuous natures and lack of communication, how plausible was it? Which gives the title the ultimate mystery: could Romeo and Juliet have discovered this Clever-Thought-Twist© for themselves, and as a result, made better decisions?

III. **The Future of Science** (page 183) - The student used the title to foreshadow his conclusion. This essay is mostly an historical journey through the innovation of scientific techniques. To title an historical essay as a forecast for the future, is a bold move. It generates suspense throughout the essay as the reader/grader attempts to figure out how the writer will deliver on his prediction.

RESPONSE A. **Roll Over Fluffy!** (page 157) - The student chooses the dog's unique ability to be trained by verbal command as the key factor through which dogs deliver superior value. Therefore, it just makes sense to emphasize the power of trainability by highlighting the cat's inability to perform. Here the title proposes that a pet owner could issue the verbal command to their cat, *"roll over"* and then watch it roll over; a trick, by the way, which most of us have seen dogs perform routinely.

The key to writing catchy titles is to weave their meaning with elements of the thesis while keeping them as short as possible. Consider how much more effective short is when comparing the two possible titles for Essay II, page 176: **Aircraft Carriers, Battleships, Cruisers and Destroyers in the US Navy** verses **Task Force**. Not only is **Task Force** a short and powerful expression, it summarizes the key benefit derived from building ships of different designs and capabilities. Additionally, the brevity of a two-word title supports the need to meet the time constraints we experience while taking live tests.

How to Put Style in the Idea Stack©

Happily, most of our deep thinking and heavy work is done once we sequence our Idea Stack©. Certainly, when writing we will take the effort to describe each idea thoroughly, support it with facts, details, and proof, and then explain why it is important – and that is work. However, we aspire to do more than this; we aspire to produce engaging writing that captures the reader's attention. While writing from an Idea Stack©, we use the following devices to create our own unique writing style:
- **Clever-Thought-Twists©**
- **Diagrams**
- **Tables**
- **Stories**

Here's how:

- **Clever-Thought-Twists©** – Why not continue to use this interest-generating device from time to time throughout our essay to introduce our discussion about each idea?

- **Diagrams** – Years ago, my sister Becky experienced serious test anxiety while preparing for her Biology exam at Worcester State College. The chapter about how cells store and release energy did not make sense to her. She became distraught over the possibility of failing the class. Becky decided to memorize three key pages word for word. As luck would have it, the professor chose to test this concept with an essay question. When Becky got to the essay question, she wrote an introduction, wrote how a cell manufactured energy from memory by repeating what was in the text word for word and summarized with a brief conclusion. The approach seemed to work well until the next class period when the professor returned the exams. Becky did not receive hers. Instead, she was told to stay after class, at which time the following conversation occurred:

Professor: *Do you know why you didn't get your test back?*

Becky: *No, I have no idea.*

Professor: *Can you think of anything that would be wrong with it?*

Becky: *No, I thought my test was fine.*

Professor: *Well, you cheated!*

Becky: *Cheated, how can you say that? I have never cheated in my life. Why would I cheat in your class?*

Professor: *I can prove it. I have a copy of your test, and you can see right here, by comparing it to the text, page 86, that you copied down every word of it when I stepped out of the room during the exam.*

Becky: *Oh that! That is ridiculous! I memorized that page. Here I can prove it to you, and I will do it by showing you that I also memorized pages 85 and 87.*

Becky shuts the textbook and proceeds to write down page 87 word for word to the astonishment of the professor...

Becky: *See, I have the chapter memorized. Now if you don't believe me, I'll reproduce pages 85 and 86, but I think you can see we are wasting each other's time.*

Professor: *No, I believe you. But, I have one more question for you, why on earth would you go through all the effort to memorize the chapter? Wouldn't it just have been easier to write about it in your own words?*

Becky: *No... because I don't understand it.*

Professor: *Ok, ok... I'm starting to get the picture. Hmmm, well, the good news is that you took this class pass/fail. If you are willing to come after class for some extra tutoring, and give it your best effort, I think we can get you to a passing grade by the end of the semester. However, you are going to have to promise me you will find another way to learn and answer test questions, because this rote memorization is unacceptable.*

Becky: *I will.*

By the end of the semester, Becky passed the class. I first heard this story while the family sat down around the dining room table eating dinner. Becky went on a rant about the insanity of colleges requiring courses outside her major and the folly of making a Theater major take Biology. She wanted us to lobby to change the entire curriculum of the State College. As I listened to her story, it occurred to me that although memorizing the pages in her textbook was a brilliant approach, it did not <u>achieve</u> the <u>objective</u> of <u>understanding</u> the <u>class material</u>. I wondered if

141

there was a better way, perhaps one could easily learn how a cell's metabolic process worked by drawing it out. To do this, one uses diagrams. One would simply look at a diagram, close the textbook, and draw what he could remember. Then open the book, check for accuracy, look for what he missed, then close the book and reproduce it again, this time writing down what he had missed. The next time I was preparing for an exam, I experimented with this approach. I was surprised that by the third or fourth attempt, I was able to reproduce the biology drawings at 100% accuracy. I now had a new tool. I found that I could reproduce the diagram in a few minutes, and shorten my test preparation. Memorizing a diagram by drawing it was faster than rote memorization and better because I was learning how things worked as I drew. In summary, drawing the diagram serves a dual purpose: it is a memory recall device and serves as an illustration for our essay.

PERFORMANCE SECRET #20: Draw a diagram to recall a complete set of information and to provide an illustration for your essay.

- **Tables** – Now the time we took to build an Idea Stack© for ***Dogs vs. Cats*** pays off! The Idea Stack© is a great source from which to build a table. Tables deliver three benefits. The first is to make sure our grader sees that we have accounted for every piece of information relevant to the question. The second is to show the inter-relationships of the information. Thirdly, and perhaps most elegant, is that it enables us to put more information down faster than to explain each idea in sentences. This allows us to write about the key points, and still include the minor ones with little writing expended. Remember that hitting every item on the teacher's list increases our grade. This next table is an example for the "The Dog is Better" essay in our ***Dogs vs. Cats*** response:

Characteristic	Dogs Best	Cats Best
Train a specific behavior by command	Yes	No
Perform jobs in the workplace	Yes	No
Police Work K-9	Yes	No
Provide sight for the blind	Yes	No
Protect the home and family	Yes	No
Attack burglars who break in	Yes	No
Deter crime against the family home	Yes	No
Play catch the tennis ball	Yes	No
Hang out and provide companionship	Yes	No

Notice how Dogs' characteristics all come out "Yes" while Cats' come out "No." This is a very subtle and powerful psychological presentation. After looking at this chart, how could anyone in their right mind think cats provide more value?

Cat lovers please do not give up hope because there is another side to this issue. The power of the table can also be used to your benefit: we simply choose ideas that deliver "Yes" characteristics for Cats and "No" characteristics for Dogs:

Characteristic	Cats Best	Dogs Best
Most popular pet	Yes	No
Feel soft and cuddly	Yes	No
Protect the home against rodents	Yes	No
Provide increased hygiene in neighborhood	Yes	No
Self-cleaning and grooming	Yes	No
Baby sit themselves	Yes	No
Cost nothing	Yes	No
Fewer housing covenant restrictions	Yes	No
Longer life	Yes	No

The characteristic "Playful" in the Cat's Idea Stack© was left out of the table because it delivers a Yes for both Cats and Dogs. For a more objective presentation, the student could include it.

On page 188, in **New Airport in Chicago**, the student utilized a table during a live exam to handle the immense amount of information the test question required the student to address. When asked to write a compare or contrast answer, with more than two options, adding a third option is just another vertical line in a T-View Outline©. Then building the table simply entails adding another column to the right of your first two columns. Finally, you write Yes's and No's in that third column. With a little bit of preparation and luck, your ideas in the table will match the teacher's answer key! It happens more often than you think.

PERFORMANCE SECRET #21: Use a table to show that you have accounted for the key information, to communicate the deep meaning of ideas and to cover more in less time.

- **Stories** – We use short stories, very short stories, to support our ideas. The purpose of using a story is to convince the reader on an emotional level, which often has more impact on a reader/grader than a logical argument. A story is simply a message with a beginning[1], a middle[2] and an end[3]. Notice that we can write a story with as few as three sentences. An example of a three-sentence story appears in **Roll Over, Fluffy!**, as follows:

    [1]*Additionally, cats are not known to save people in danger, yet Leo, a Jack Russell Terrier, saved four kittens by standing guard and leading the firefighters to their bed in a burning Australian home in October of 2008.* [2]*Smoke overcame the Terrier and he had to be resuscitated by firefighters.* [3]*Meanwhile, the mother cat was nowhere to be found.*

The name of the dog anchors emotion into the reader's heart, while the date and place delivers credibility. This credibility highlights the importance of being accurate and remembering details from the classroom, textbook and life all around us. (Also notice the powerful use of **Additionally/Yet**, words perfectly suited for executing the Direct Approach© found on pages 64-67).

On the other hand, there are circumstances where a paragraph-long story fits our objective better than a short one. In Essay III, **Risk**, page 180, the student utilizes three stories, each describing an event, one after the other, to illustrate the payoffs and losses of taking and not taking risks. The stories set up an everyday event to be the high-impact conclusion. Coincidently, he earned an "A" while using only a story for his conclusion. The value of using stories as a style device is, that a well-chosen story can convey a more powerful emotional message than facts or details.

PERFORMANCE SECRET #22: Use a story to deliver an idea with powerful emotional impact.

How to Put Style in the Conclusion

This is our last paragraph. We have already established our style in the prior sections of our essay – Introduction and Idea Stack©. Our reader is either engaged (engaged if we have been following **The No-Study Solution**© Game Plan) or bored and taking it out on us with a low score in red ink (if we are making it up as we go along). Our primary objective now is to drive our thesis home. It doesn't hurt to continue using style devices to kick off the conclusion as the following Clever-Thought-Twist© does in **Roll Over, Fluffy!** page 159:

"Imagine saying to your cat, "Roll Over, Fluffy!" No sane cat owner ever would, because he cannot train any cat to roll over on command. In contrast, police dogs, sight dogs, and family dogs follow commands and instincts as they deter thieves, give sight and provide companionship throughout the fabric of society."

Other times a diagram or table is more effective for covering all the pieces required to answer the test question as illustrated in **New Airport in Chicago** on page 188. Frequently, we take the straightforward approach. We restate our thesis, sprinkle in a few of our findings, and state the importance of our thesis as the student did in **Task Force** on page 178.

WARNING: One of the most common mistakes students make in the conclusion is to advance their thought process to a new insight beyond the thesis. The Conclusion is not the place to drop new insight on our grader/reader. Neither should we write a concluding statement that goes beyond what we have proved in the essay itself. That is the job of the essay. In the Conclusion, more than in any other section, it is critical that we do not lose sight of our objective – to convince the reader that our thesis is valid.

To wrap up our conclusion, we build a style device into the trifecta of thesis statement, key proof and why important. While doing so, we have the courage to take our position for the last time. We restate our thesis sentence as the truth, fact or undeniable conclusion. This will mirror the thesis in the Introduction as the student did in **What Ancient Rome Could Teach Romeo and Juliet**, pages 172 and 174. Confidence carries the day in this section. Imagine that we are an attorney making our closing argument before the jury; we never would be vague or timid. Neither would we suggest that there is a possibility of guilt: *"well, maybe my client is a little at fault, but..."* No! Rather, we would be confident in the courtroom knowing that our preceding arguments are sound. Similarly, when concluding our essay, we radiate confidence. Ironically, simply in being confident, we infuse more style in our essay than most of our classmates ever will, and by doing so – create an engaging style uniquely our own.

Readability

One aspect of our writing that has a tremendous impact on our grade is whether our teacher can actually read it! Despite being obvious, this is such a critical piece of our grade, that it deserves our attention for the next few pages. It is time for a personal inventory. Ask yourself these questions:
- *How legible is my handwriting?*
- *How much effort is the grader going to put out attempting to decipher what I wrote?*
- *How tired is she going to get struggling to read my handwriting?*

The truth is that readability influences our grade. Yes, I know that readability is not technically a word, but with the current beer commercials adding drinkability to the popular American lexicon, perhaps "readability" is not too far behind official acceptance as a word.

Teachers and graders are human. They react to annoyances in a predictable way – the way any human being would, which is to take it out on the next person's paper they grade. Unfortunately, if your teacher has difficulty reading your essay, she will take it out on your grade. I learned this from an experience during my junior year in High School English class. Coincidently, my instructor, Mr. Smiles, had also been my teacher for freshman English. This year-plus break from him as my teacher created the event that revealed the power of readability.

While a junior, Mr. Smiles said to me:

"When I first saw your handwriting freshman year I felt so sorry for you not being able to write legibly. I thought there might have been something wrong with you. It just didn't make for easy reading and your grades reflected it.

I am sorry about the low grade I gave you freshman year, if I had known that you broke your hand playing football, I never would have graded you so harshly.

You really gave me a shock around the holidays. The take-home essay you passed in was written in excellent penmanship. Your penmanship was so different from what you had done so far – even the slope had changed from that of a left-handed person to a right-handed person – I was sure that you had someone else write your midterm exam for you.

So, the next day, I watched you closely in class, hovering around your desk, waiting for you to take some notes. When I glanced down at your notes, the words were in the same handwriting as your mid-term exam. I had never seen anyone change his handwriting overnight, which is why I asked you out of the blue, how did you write that?

Mark, if you had <u>told</u> <u>me</u> at the beginning of the year that you had broken your writing hand, maybe we could have <u>worked</u> <u>something</u> <u>out</u>. I gave you <u>much</u> <u>better</u> <u>grades</u> after that."

Remember that when we show up for school, we are simply walking into a game – the game of Performance. <u>We</u> choose to make it a game. People, who play games with the goal to win or to have fun, keep looking for better ways to play that game. As I heard Mr. Smiles speak, I was <u>listening</u> for <u>actions</u> I could <u>take</u> to improve my game. I am always listening for ways to improve my performance. Through listening and then and asking, *"How can I use this experience?"* I came up with two actions I took into the rest of my school career:

- First, be in communication with my instructor… especially whenever unusual events in my personal life interfere with my ability to perform.
- Second, handwriting influences my grade significantly so write clearly on tests from now on.

Happily, we can improve our handwriting by simply changing our approach with one or more of the following techniques:

1. **Double Spacing**
2. **Slowing Down**
3. **Changing Our Angle**
4. **Printing**

(1) Double Spacing – This means skipping a line between each written line. The space between written lines opens up our essay visually making it easier to read. This is especially true for cursive, where letters such as "g" and "q" go below the line. These letters interfere with the writing on the line below. Years later, I used the double space technique as I wrote my response to **New Airport in Chicago** in my blue test booklet. A reproduction of the original appears on the next page to illustrate this technique:

III Essay

Mayor Daley is faced with a tough decision given three choices and there is competition among airports for traffic and freight so the airport must be put in a location where Demand can support an airport operating at the ✓ lowest point on its survival curve.

Long RUN Costs

· Short run Costs have two components:

(2) Slow Down – Counter-intuitive to the way most students think, this strategy takes nothing more than awareness. Imagine what would happen if you slowed down your writing just for one essay test and focused on making your letters more clear. Watch the pen move slower as the mind directs the hand to form each cursive letter correctly. You can improve your handwriting overnight by slowing down. This is a surprisingly easy and effective approach. Experiment with it. You may be quite happy with the results.

(3) Change the Angle – How many of us have played around with our handwriting lately? Oftentimes our handwriting clears up instantaneously when we tilt our slanted cursive to nearly vertical. For most of us, writing more perpendicular to the lines is an easy way to generate penmanship that is more legible. Coincidently, this technique often slows down our handwriting, thereby achieving technique #2 while focusing on technique #3. Changing the angle is two results for one effort technique.

(4) Print – Seldom does anyone dictate that we must use cursive. If our handwriting is unsalvageable after double spacing, slowing down and changing our angle, do not despair. We can always print. After all, it is where we started years ago when we began forming letters with a pencil in kindergarten. Many of the engineering and architectural disciplines require this most clear method of hand-written communication. Obviously, the down side to this approach is that it is a significantly slower process. Therefore, there is some risk to this technique. If we choose to print, the THINK and STAGE phases of our Game Plan become ever so much more important – due to the slower writing speed of printing, we now must think through how to communicate our ideas with fewer words and be economical with our writing style.

PERFORMANCE SECRET #23: Clean up your handwriting by double spacing, slowing down, changing the angle or printing.

3-C. Linking Writing With The Clock

Making Time Work

Nothing is more frustrating while writing our essay than to hear the words *"Time's up! Pass your tests to the front of the room."* As we perfect our use of the Timing Ladder© we will not fear these words any more. Writing high scoring essays is a three-skill sport. The first skill is flowing our thoughts into a model as we write; the second skill is engaging the reader with style and the third skill is managing our time.

Clock management makes a powerful and convincing conclusion possible. In **Dogs vs. Cats**, the teacher gives us 15 minutes for the question. If the test begins at 3:00 pm in the afternoon, we jot down our Idea Stack© until 3:03 at which point we shift to writing the Introduction. We start our Idea Stack© at 3:04 and begin our Conclusion at 3:13. We stop by 3:15. Once we are familiar with the layout of the timing ladder, we can jot down the shift point times in the margins some place where the teacher will not notice them: 3:03, 3:04, 3:13 and 3:15. We may not even need to draw the lines, just have the times or the blocks of time in our head. For this scenario, we think, *"I'm timing it 1/9/2."*

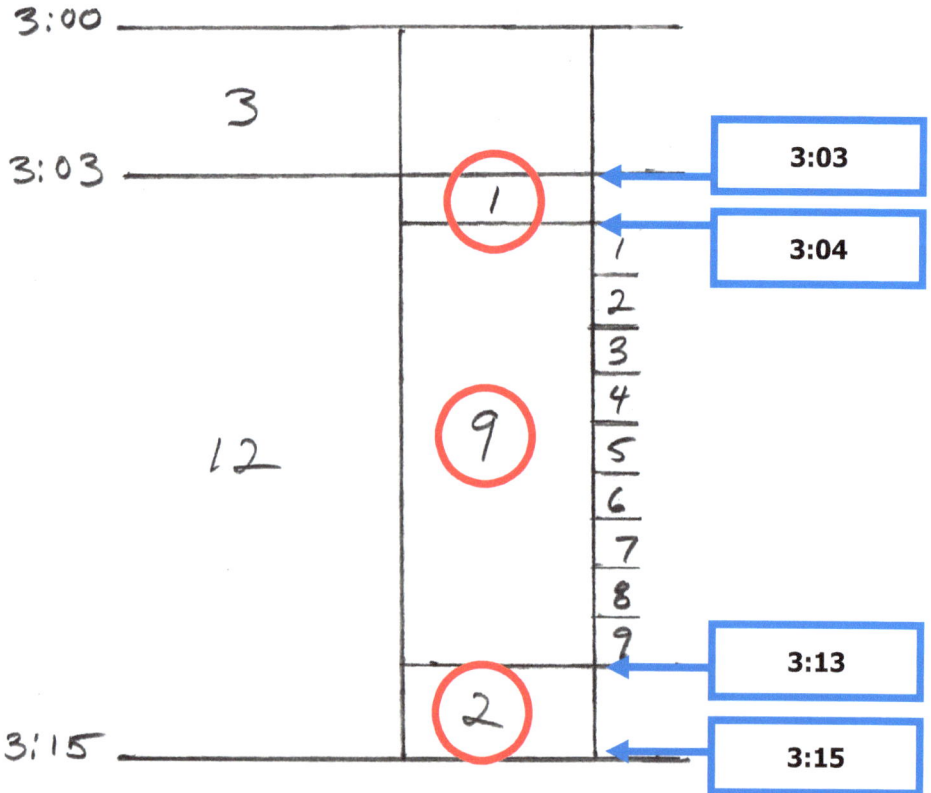

Counting time made sense to a basketball champion, and it just <u>makes sense</u> for us when we play <u>our</u> game. After all, time is the one element we control completely. Being in control is a satisfying feeling. Now that we have made The No-Study Solution©'s Secrets, Strategies and Models part of playing our game, let's revisit the *"Gap Between the Teacher and the Test"* to see just how far we have come in leaping the gap.

4. CROSS THE GAP!

In this section, you will:
- **Get the road map for crossing the gap**
- **Believe that you can prove either side of a question**
- **Discover ways to know what will be on the test**

The One Thing

Now that we have spent a fair amount of time together and you have been exposed to all aspects of **The No-Study Solution**© for writing essays, what is the one thing you could take away from this book that would improve your grades the most?

The one thing is to have a Game Plan and to follow that Game Plan. To assist the student with remembering the Game Plan we have put together three views of it. Any one of them will work. The first is a conceptual view showing how the plan and tools work together (this page). The second is a detailed road map of the system laying out each step with words and pictures (next page). A third view, which is a flow chart of the writing process appears on page 102. A person can write a persuasive and high scoring essay from any one of these views depending upon their familiarity with the system. Feel free to commit to memory whichever view works best for you and use it in your exams.

The No-Study Solution© for Writing Essays - Concept View

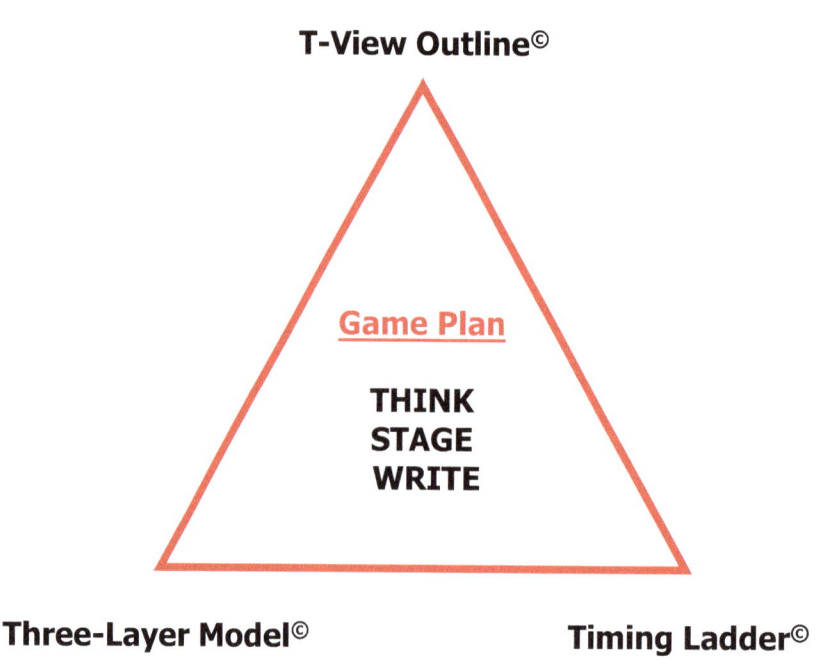

It is interesting to compare the detail on this page and the following page with our first presentation of them on pages 23-24. We have come a long way in Knowing how to improve our performance!

The No-Study Solution© for Writing Essays - Strategy View

The Game Plan:

1. THINK:
- Think Up Ideas
- De-Bug Ideas
- Defuse Counter-Ideas

2. STAGE:
- Write Thesis Statement
- Sequence Ideas
- Divide Time

3. WRITE:
- Use Three-Layer Model©
  - INTRODUCTION
    - **H**ello Sentence
    - **I**ssue Sentence
    - **T**hesis Sentence
  - IDEA 1
    - Describe
    - Proof
    - Importance
  - IDEA 2
    - Describe
    - Proof
    - Importance
  - IDEA 3
    - Describe
    - Proof
    - Importance
  - CONCLUSION
    - Thesis
    - Ideas Covered
    - Importance
- Engage the Reader
  - Clever-Thought-Twists©
  - Tables, Diagrams, Charts
- Link Time to Clock

The Elements:

T-View Outline©

DOGS BEST	CATS BEST
2 – WORK	– SOFT ☺
4 – SIGHT DOGS	– KILL RATS
3 – POLICE K-9	– SELF CLEANING
8 – BITE THIEVES	– BABY SIT SELF
~~5 – RACING~~	– BUY FOR FREE
9 – PLAY CATCH	– HAVE A LOT
6 – PROTECT FAMILY	– PLAYFUL
~~LIVE 10-14 YEARS~~	– 12-16 YEAR LIFE
10 – HANG OUT	
~~WALK 2x A DAY~~	– MOST POPULAR
1 – TRAINABLE	– LESS SHEDDING
7 – BARK LOUD	

Timing Ladder©

3		
	1	
12	9	1
		2
		3
		4
		5
		6
		7
		8
		9
	2	

The Three-Layer Model

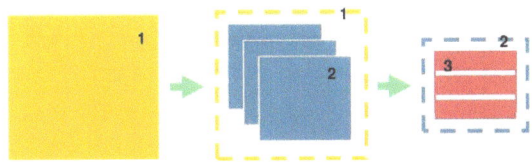

The No-Study Solution! – Writing Essays

The Power to Prove Either Side

One of the major benefits of using a T-View Outline© is that we have the opportunity to think through writing two essays instead of just one. The T-View Outline© provides a projected view of how each side of the essay will turn out. It provides the ability to weigh the pros and cons. It enables us to write from a broader perspective – perhaps even be objective! We will now present a response from each side of **Dogs vs. Cats** to illustrate this flexibility.

TEST QUESTION: *Consider the relative value of a cat verses a dog as a pet. Which pet generates the most value to both the pet owner individually and society as a whole?*

DOGS BEST	CATS BEST
2 – WORK	– SOFT ☺
4 – SIGHT DOGS	– KILL RATS
3 – POLICE K-9	– SELF CLEANING
8 – BITE THIEVES	– BABY SIT SELF
~~5 – RACING~~	– BUY FOR FREE
9 – PLAY CATCH	– HAVE A LOT
6 – PROTECT FAMILY	– PLAYFUL
~~– LIVE 10-14 YEARS~~	– 12-16 YEAR LIFE
10 – HANG OUT	– MOST POPULAR
~~– WALK 2X A DAY~~	– LESS SHEDDING
1 – TRAINABLE	
7 – BARK LOUD	

RESPONSE A: *Dogs vs. Cats* - The "Dog is Better" Essay

Roll Over, Fluffy!

A cursory look at Ancient Egyptian art reveals that dogs participated at the forefront of their military and leadership activities, yet today, nearly 5,000 years later, the question of whether a dog or a cat delivers the most value still lingers in some people's minds. From the past to the present, Dogs have been trained to perform specific and complex tasks that humans simply cannot do. Dogs deliver superior value to society over cats because people can train them to follow spoken commands.

Among domesticated animals, dogs uniquely possess the ability to be trained to follow spoken commands. We find people training dogs commercially and privately. Commercially, police dogs are trained as puppies to follow the commands: sit, down, stay, heel and come here. Later, as adults, these dogs are trained to attack criminals and retreat, sniff out weapons and drugs, and detain suspects. Privately, dog owners train their personal pets to walk on a leash, sit, stay, come, hunt, play fetch, catch the flying disc, ride skateboards, jump on snowboards and retrieve newspapers. These activities prove that dogs can be trained to follow spoken commands.

Today we have technology available that supports livestock management. Fencing, tagging, branding and computers assist farmers to raise cattle, sheep, and other livestock, track their locations, and manage their "harvesting" as a profitable business. This was not always the case. For centuries, Collies, Australian Shepherds, Great Pyrenees and other breeds provided protection from predators and thieves, while assisting with daily tasks such as movement and containment. However, today's technological innovations still do not compare to the sophistication of a herding dog. We see this regularly at livestock herding competitions where dogs move sheep through obstacle courses instructed merely by the sound of a whistle. In these trials, a dog is measured by time, course accuracy, and location of animals at the end of the course. Nothing new, the first recorded sheepdog trials occurred in Wales, in 1873. This advanced herding "technology" has been available to society for thousands of years, a result of the dog's ability to be trained by language.

Police work is a valuable benefit that dogs provide to society today. Despite the highly advanced state of technology, Police dogs still provide services unmatched by any other source. While performing police fieldwork, a K-9 German Shepherd can sense the direction of a fleeing suspect beyond the range of portable infrared devices. Additionally, dogs can detect the presence of suspects invisible to the human eye. Once apprehended, the police dog will attack or stand down on command. The dog will also watch the suspect as the officer approaches and will warn or respond as necessary should the suspect attempt to flee or draw a weapon. Additionally, Police dogs generate more fear in most people than a second officer does. I observed this personally in a ride-along with a K-9 team. Police dogs are the most cost-effective and pervasive detector of explosive devices and illegal drugs in airport security today. Overseas, the US military has deployed 70 dogs in Afghanistan with plans to increase their numbers to 219 in July 2010. In one month, these dogs discovered 20 unexploded bombs, saving the lives of our troops. The security work police dogs perform is significant for two reasons. First, they often perform jobs humans cannot perform. Humans cannot follow the trail of a missing person the way a Bloodhound can. Second, they can take on tasks too dangerous for humans. War dogs can identify hidden explosive devices that humans cannot see, thereby preserving soldiers' limbs and lives. All these security benefits at home and abroad are possible due to a dog's ability to be trained by human communication. In today's financially challenged environment, it is vital to utilize low-cost and effective solutions such as these police and military dogs to maximize the public good.

Golden Retrievers, Weimaraners and other working dogs are trained to be the eyes of the blind. Not only do they obey the spoken words of their visually challenged owners, these dogs are also trained to handle the challenges and obstacles of moving their owner through his physical life. Trainers who can see have pre-programmed the dog's mental and emotional systems. Once matched to their owner, these dogs provide safe passage through crosswalks, down busy streets, up elevators and through everyday obstacles. This is important because the seeing eye dog gives the sight challenged individual a freedom to move through life unavailable by any other means, even if he or she could afford a cadre of full-time hired help.

Cats on the other hand, are seldom trained to follow verbal commands of any significance other than being called to eat. Hence, the popular phrase, "herding cats," was first introduced into mainstream culture in a famous TV commercial, and humorously presents cowboys herding cats in contrast to the more common mental picture of cowboys herding cattle. The implication is that cattle are more manageable than cats. The commercial is a poignant reminder of how little value cats can provide to society outside the home, because they cannot be trained to perform tasks.

Dogs contribute to public safety across the widest spectrum by protecting families from intruders. Even if the electrical power goes out, the family dog still knows a burglar is out there. Burglars do not trust a vicious and crazy dog in close quarters. Their residential break-in comes to a halt the moment the dog attacks. The thieves are now on the defensive – running for their lives. In any *event, secrecy is lost, the chance of being caught rises, and it is no surprise that a dog's mere presence deters crime.*

Additionally, cats are not known to save people in danger, yet Leo, a Jack Russell Terrier, saved four kittens by standing guard and leading the firefighters to their bed in a burning Australian home in October of 2008. Smoke overcame the Terrier and he had to be resuscitated by firefighters. Meanwhile, the mother cat was nowhere to be found. This selfless act by a dog demonstrates that it is always ready to deliver value, trained or untrained; the dog instinctively knows how to save people and other animals in danger. This example underscores how broad a dog's value to society is, spanning both loyalty and courage.

For some people, public health is a bigger issue than public safety. These folks suggest cats provide the benefit of eliminating an unsanitary rat population. However, this argument overlooks the fact that a simple purchase of rat poison at the store for $18 will eliminate rats, while there is no low-cost way of keeping intruders from breaking into one's home the way a dog does. Given that there are low cost ways to achieve the benefits of cats while, few, if any expensive technologies can replace dogs, it is clear that dogs deliver superior value to the public good. One wonders if the mother cat of the four kittens in the burning house mentioned above was out hunting rats while her babies were in danger.

Family dogs of most breeds or mixtures can be trained to catch a ball, return flying discs, retrieve newspapers, ride skateboards and travel on boat or plane. Regardless, of the type of dog considered, most dogs can be trained to be housebroken, stay in a geographical area, and behave in an acceptable manner. As a dog follows the commands of its owner, it blends in with the family and becomes part of its social dynamic. Just the other day, the writer witnessed an English Bulldog standing on a skateboard, towed by its owner riding a bicycle. Only the leash connected the two. The writer clocked the tandem traveling at 7 miles per hour. This unique match of dog to owner in temperament and activities is, ultimately, the characteristic of dogs that enables them to deliver superior value to pet owners over cats.

Imagine saying to your cat, "Roll Over, Fluffy!" No sane cat owner ever would, because he cannot train any cat to roll over on command. In contrast, police dogs, sight dogs and family dogs follow commands and instincts as they deter thieves, give sight and provide companionship throughout the fabric of society. Ultimately, it is a dog's superior intelligence and evolution, perhaps even influenced by coexisting with man since the days of Ancient Egypt, which allows dogs to learn and follow spoken commands. Their ability to perform beneficial actions even when not supervised is the final proof that a dog delivers superior value to society as a whole and to people individually.

RESPONSE B: *Dogs vs. Cats* - (The "Cat is Better" Essay)

Cats Rule, Dogs Drool

The age-old controversy over which is the better domestic pet — a dog or a cat — is easily answered. The only reason it persists is the existence of outspoken opinionated pet owners of the opposite side. For companionship, health, and ease, the cat is the most obvious choice.

From ancient times to the present, the cat is held as the more intelligent, wise, and listening sort of creature. The Chinese and Japanese cultures, as well as other Asian cultures (like Burmese and Siamese) held cats in high regard; pets belonged to royalty, and were even bred for use in the palaces. There are European tales from hundreds of years ago of smart cats or enchanted cats (The Enchanted Cat — by the Brothers Grimm, Puss in Boots – by Hans Christian Anderson). The Egyptians were known to worship cats, and to have spent time with them such that when the Egyptians died they wanted their cats to be buried with them because they could not live in the afterworld without them. It was assumed a hardship to run a farm in Europe or colonial America without cats. The same was assumed by pioneers settling the West. In 20th century America, there have been many famous cats of companionship in popular comic strips and cartoon series. Within these comic adventures, we see spoofs on the pet being wiser than the human, the pet being more human than the human, and often the cat being smarter than the dog. While the cat has the human's situation figured out for him, the dog is drooling on the rug, causing a new situation for the human to address. Of course, these are fictional presentations, but if they were not based in real situations and natural tendencies, they would not "ring true" and would not "sell" in the international comedic market. As companions, cats can provide a longer relationship since their lifespan is 12-16 years, whereas a dog's lifespan is 10-14. Also, to start up a relationship is much less expensive as cats can usually be obtained for free.

In the health angle, cats hold a "slam-dunk" position. They shed hair less. They usually have less hair to shed as well – due to their size. Cats wiped out the black plague in Europe several centuries ago. There was a slight revival of the same plague in the West near Mexico about a decade ago. The same thing happened: rats and mice needed to be killed quickly and in large numbers, as they were carriers. Suddenly the cat overcame the dog as the premier choice in that area. Cats are very clean animals and only improve their environment. They wash all sorts of things and actually get things clean. How many dogs have you known that lick a wound or itch for hours and still look like a mangy dog when he is through? Yet, almost all cats successfully self-groom and look as good as if they had come from a grooming shop.

The final winning aspect is ease. The Animal Control Officers in every county could uphold this one. Dogs need to be kept out of the cold, but they cannot be kept in the house for too long (more than 8 hours) or that would be assumed cruelty as well, since the owner needs to take them out to go to the bathroom. If kept outside, dogs must be tethered, but there are restrictions as to what sort of a collar and what sort of a "run" or "lead" he is allowed to be tied to. Length is also a tricky consideration. Dogs have more energy than cats and therefore are harder to confine, entertain and exercise. Now, contrasting with cats, cats can spend all their time indoors if convenient for the owner, because cats use a litter box which has to be dealt with only once a week, which means that a cat owner deals with the issue of excretion once a week rather than two to three times per day. Temperature is not so much a problem, as cats find ways to limit their activity in order to adjust to extremes, with even a sub-hibernating system and the greater ability to take a catnap anytime, anywhere. There are laws and ordinances in almost every town regarding cats and dogs, and the laws are always stiffer on dogs: an owner can have more cats than dogs, has to license the dog, but not the cat, while dogs require rabies shots. Cats are calmer and get into less trouble than dogs, and even entertain themselves. When going on vacation, pet owners have to rent a kennel or hire a sitter for a dog, whereas a cat can be attended to only every three days if enough provisions are set out.

Dog owners may object to the above, pointing out that a dog is more trainable, but with closer research, one will find that cats are very trainable: this writer has trained eleven cats to defecate in a human toilet, and one to flush the toilet when finished. Cats are trained to eat in a certain place, just like dogs, or to obey certain household rules. As far as playing with owners, cats play in ways that are more docile: they do not usually catch flying discs, but they will chase strings and roll around just as much as dogs. While it is true that cats are not put to work sniffing out drugs and patrolling with police officers, the work cats do around farms is every bit as important.

In closing, we see why the age-old controversy over which is the better domestic pet — a dog or a cat — is easily answered. For companionship from the ancients to the comic strip readers, for health from the plague to rabies, or for ease such that the owner could actually go on a vacation, the cat is the most obvious choice.

Anticipate What's on the Test

There is no exact science to knowing what our teacher will put on the next test. However, an instructor on the other side of town, teaching the same subject, on the same level, can guess what will be on the test with a high degree of accuracy. Why? Because every topic is defined by key principles and concepts. Anticipating what will be on an exam is simply a matter of identifying these key concepts and looking at the different applications of those concepts. The key principles or concepts do not change from one classroom to the next on the same subject. This means that if we can find a way to hone in on these key concepts and play with their different applications, we will anticipate what is on the next test to a large extent. Therefore, cheating aside, anticipating what is on the test is an art rather than a science.

We now present two strategies with which to do this art. The first is to put together a T-View Outline©. The second is to find the most significant aspect of a concept, the **Point of Leverage**.

- **1st Approach — Building a T-View Outline©** — Now that we have mastered how to build a T-View Outline© and realize that we will likely be using one to organize our Thinking on the next essay test, why not start early and practice building a few T-View Outline©s?

We practice by looking at the class material, building a T-View Outline© as quickly as we can, analyzing the outline, sequencing it, and then building another outline from a different point of view and analyzing that. Getting together with friends, rather than preparing alone, is a powerful way to stimulate learning and discover new thoughts. Group preparation, as long as you focus and do not over socialize, reduces the time it takes to prepare and provides a more thorough learning experience.

- **2nd Approach — Finding the Point of Leverage** — The most influential aspect of the course material is often the Point of Leverage. There can be multiple points of leverage in a "system." However, one point will outperform all the others in making things happen with the least effort. In many ways, this entire book is based upon this premise. Points of Leverage are also the keys to winning most games.

The Point of Leverage shows up as either the maximum point of power and strength, or the spot of greatest weakness or zone of vulnerability. When an opponent faced Achilles on the battlefield in Ancient Greece, the Point of Leverage for the attacker was Achilles' heel. This body part was the only place where Achilles was vulnerable. Eventually someone figured this out or perhaps just got lucky and hit his heel with an arrow by accident. Regardless, the indestructible warrior died from the wound. The value of finding Points of Leverage in school courses is that this is where the teacher often places the most emphasis. Consequently, it is here where you can earn the grade points other students in your class typically miss.

Whether we are looking at military combat or any other "system" such as physics, astronomy, social dynamics, business or human behavior, there are going to be Points of Leverage in the way things work. The way things work is not the same everywhere in these systems. The spot where we can affect the biggest change with the least effort is what we want to find. Points of Leverage are often the most significant aspect of the course we are taking. Seldom are we unaware of these points; however we often overlook these concepts believing that a superficial awareness is sufficient – rather than digging in and really grasping the concept. The safe play is to be able to explain how the Point of Leverage works. If we know how it works, then we can apply it to any situation the teacher dreams up for the test.

During the 1800's, a brilliant soldier nearly conquered all of Europe – twice! Napoleon did this by using a few simple strategies based upon the concept of leverage. The strategies came into play when he engaged an enemy army on the battlefield. Napoleon usually commanded a smaller army. This typically happened because multiple countries would band together in an attempt to stop Napoleon. Knowing that the soldiers from opposing armies frequently spoke different languages, Napoleon looked for the place where the different armies joined. He attacked this point because it was where the soldiers would have to communicate to defend effectively, but could not communicate because they spoke different languages.

Unlike today where soldiers wear uniforms that blend in with nature, armies in Napoleon's day fought wearing brightly colored uniforms: reds, yellows, blues, purples, whites and fancy gold trim. The colors made it easy for the commanders to see and move their soldiers around in large groups. However, these colors also revealed to the opponent how the army was put together. Simply by looking across the field at the color of the soldier's uniforms, Napoleon could see where one country's soldiers ended and another's began. By knowing the country, Napoleon also knew the languages the soldiers spoke.

History has shown that when Napoleon attacked the place where opposing armies from different nations joined, the defense broke down rapidly. Once Napoleon had attacked from the front and punched a hole in the enemy line, he would then turn to the right and to the left and assault each of the two armies on their sides – points of even greater leverage! No army could survive an assault on its' vulnerable side and quickly surrendered. Napoleon had won another battle because he exploited one Point of Leverage that opened up a second point of even greater leverage. Therefore, one could say that Napoleon won most of his battles due to a superior grasp of the Point of Leverage.

Similarly, when we correctly identify the Point of Leverage in our school courses, we will earn higher grades than we do today, perhaps even higher than we expect. In order to do this, we must know how the "system" works and identify what our teacher emphasizes. If our teacher thinks something is a big deal, it probably is a Point of Leverage. We use questions like these to discover the Point of Leverage:

- *What makes this work?*
- *What is the one thing I need to understand in this class – which if I do not – will kill my grade?*
- *What is the key principle this topic builds upon?*
- *What concepts in this class do your students have the most difficult time handling on tests?*

Keep asking these questions, even if it means asking a brother or sister, friend, neighbor, strange student or heaven forbid – even your instructor! This is no time to be shy or worry about what someone in your class will think if you ask a "dumb" question. Let them get the lower score. Your goal is to score the most points possible, so remember that somebody out there knows... especially classmates who took the course the year before. Someone out there can explain it to you in a way that makes sense. Keep asking questions until you fully grasp the concept.

As we ask questions and find the Point of Leverage, we gain the ability to handle "trick-questions" and even handle situations that "haven't been covered in class." The more questions we ask, the more prepared we are for the exam.

PERFORMANCE SECRET #24: Find the Point of Leverage by asking the question, *"What makes this work?"*

The Last Conclusion

When we write essays from a Game Plan and put our thoughts together in a strategic manner, we end up achieving better grades. Students who earn better grades get access to better schools. Graduates from better schools receive offers for better jobs. People working in better jobs have more opportunities for money, freedom, challenge and fulfillment. Students who start their own businesses with excellent math, writing and computer skills are more successful than those who do not.

How can I support this point of view? I lived it. An essay I wrote in High School resulted in earning a half-tuition scholarship for college. As I developed and applied the concepts in this book, my college GPA rose every year – from B to B+, B+ to A-, and A- to A. As employers came on campus and started screening students based upon GPA, I was able to land interviews with IBM and Proctor & Gamble, two of the most desirable companies to work for at that time.

In fact, my transcript did not even match the stated degree and minimum credit hour requirements of my first employer, International Business Machines Corporation (IBM). They hired me because I demonstrated better skills than students who had the "right" courses. Here is how that happened.

In my senior year, I was excited about Transportation, but there were no courses in the subject offered at my university. Therefore, I went to my favorite Economics professor and asked him how I could get started now – instead of waiting for graduate school. He suggested we design an independent study class around the "Transportation Problem." So virtually all of my credit hours in my last semester were wrapped up into this one-on-one research project with my professor. I spent weeks in the library reading graduate level texts on the "Transportation Problem" and researching professional Economic Journals on the effects of the most current legislation in transportation, the Deregulation of the Trucking Industry in 1980.

Soon IBM comes to town for a career day, and I put on my best suit and tie, comb my hair and walk over to the huge auditorium. After three hours, I am almost out of résumés with no interviews. I can see how to get an interview. As I wait in a line, students up in front of me hand their résumé to a person in a blue suit. The suit looks up, smiles and has an animated conversation with the student. Occasionally, the suit pulls out an interview calendar and writes the student's name in a time slot. Each time I have that conversation, the suit says, *"you do not meet our requirements."* Tucson wants **"Accounting Majors,"** not minors like me – Salt Lake City demanded **"Business Majors,"** not Economics majors, like me – Raleigh wants **"Finance Majors"**, not finance classes like mine.

Frustrating! I have spent three years of my life in college and I cannot even get an interview from one of the blue suits.

What's this? People are leaving the huge auditorium. The suits are packing up and leaving the building. I glance at my watch, oh, it is lunchtime…

Do I even come back? Hmmm… Looks like there are two people left in the hall, me and… Who is this at the end of the hall? There is a man sitting behind a table eating his lunch. He is wearing a blue suit, white shirt and red silk tie. The sign on the table says, **"MBA's, San Jose, CA."** (I have a BS).

Mark: "Are you looking for MBA's or someone who knows a lot about how business works?"

Hiring Manager: "What do you know about business?"

Mark: Well, I know about the Deregulation Act of 1980! It is creating opportunities for trucking companies to compete on price, and that this competition is leading to lower costs for manufacturing firms. With lower shipping costs, manufacturers can be more profitable and invest more in higher quality products."

Hiring Manager: "Tell me more about that!"

I share the insights I am learning researching the "Transportation Problem." The man is putting down his newspaper now, and the unfinished sandwich is going back inside the brown paper bag. We are talking about his business, some kind of huge complex with many buildings, a golf course, a manufacturing line, clean rooms for silicon chips, parts coming in from all over the country, shipping out to all known locations in the civilized world: New York, Japan, Hong Kong. Wow! I start telling him how the costs of these transportation services he is buying will change, and he interrupts me…

Hiring Manager: "You have most of this right, but we don't work that way here in my Division, we are telling the industry what we want to pay and getting them to compete for our business."

Mark: "How do you do that?"

The blue suit is explaining his interaction with companies in the Trucking Industry: Viking, Yellow Freight, Conway, Old Dominion, Best Way, Ryder, and ABF. This is real world stuff, not the research and law journals I am reading in the Harold B. Lee library at all hours of the night.

Mark: *"Do you mind if I quote you on that in my research paper? I would really like to include this."*

Hiring Manager: *"No... not at all. What is this research paper for?"*

Mark: *"This is my senior paper on the Transportation Problem."*

I am writing frantically now in my notebook, asking questions, getting his name – Dave Hartman, title – Plant Manager and location of interview – Provo, UT as I envision a true researcher would. In my peripheral vision, I am aware of people filing back into the auditorium now; an hour has flown by as we talked.

Hiring Manager: *"I need to get back to work, but before I do, are you free tomorrow for an interview?"*

At last, I saw my name written into a time slot! During that interview, Dave Hartmann asked for a copy of my research paper. Weeks of work, asking questions, reading journals and writing had paid off. Although he was not looking to add anyone with a BS to his Transportation Department, Dave flew me out to California for a site visit, introduced me to the team and presented a job offer. IBM had been on the cover of Fortune magazine that fall as the best company to work for in America, and naturally, I accepted.

Hiring Manager: *"I am looking forward to seeing what you will do here in San Jose. When I went to BYU, I wanted to come away with an MBA graduate to put into our management development program. You were the only student I spoke with who knew about what we do here in Distribution. Instead, I hired you! Good Luck! And have a successful career!"*

The most amazing aspect of this story is that a bachelor's degree graduate took an MBA hiring slot. Somewhere in that university, an MBA graduate accepted a position at a company ranked lower than #1 by Fortune magazine and he had studied two years longer. I achieved my dream, which was a career in the Transportation Industry and something more. I was working for the most prestigious company in the USA. This is the payoff of using the techniques in this book, especially PERFORMANCE SECRET #3: Achieve common sense by being <u>curious</u> and asking, *"How does this work?"*

In the first chapter (-1) of this book I say, "**KNOWING, PREPARING,** and **PERFORMING** are the three skills used to leap the gap between the teacher and the test – **not studying**." I <u>knew</u> that I wanted a job in the Transportation Industry. I also <u>knew</u> how to put together my research paper with clear and powerful writing. Unknowingly, I had prepared months for that interview with IBM. The IBM Distribution Division that Dave Hartmann ran focused on truck transportation of computer parts. When it came to performing, all I had to do was ask one question, *"Are you looking for MBA's or someone who knows a lot about how business works?"* After that, it was just a conversation and being curious about how his business worked.

You have now read this book. You now have at your fingertips the tools and strategies it takes to write powerful essays and communicate persuasively. The knowing how of leaping the gap is handled. The preparing is all that is left for you to do. So if you are not motivated to prepare, what can you do?

You look at why you are not inspired. What is missing in your vision of your life that allows you to get distracted from your dreams and pursuit of your goals? Did you leave out the things that you truly love and inspire you? You are going to leave school and end up somewhere doing something. The question is ***what*** *are you preparing* ***for***?

Knowing what you want in life puts the rest of your activities in perspective. No effort is too much work when it leads to a career you love, participating in an adventure you dream about, or living a life that excites you. The alternative is being bored out of your mind and depressed – for a lifetime.

This leaves you with only one more question to ask – **Do I really know what I want?** A key to success is being clear about what you want and taking advantage of the opportunities around you right now. Given that you are a student, the fastest way to get what you want is to gain some skills by doing well in school. The skills you gain will open doors to opportunities for you just as it did for me.

Knowing what you want will drive you to improve your skills and take advantage of all the strategies and tools in **The No-Study Solution**©. On each successive test, you will get better. As you improve, your confidence will grow. You will experience being in control. After a while, you will look forward to essay tests because you excel at them. One day you will realize that you have leaped the **Gap Between the Teacher and the Test** – and in that moment, you will realize that you are one of the smart people. Then you will know that you can do or be anything that you want to be in life.

PERFORMANCE SECRET #25: Know what you want.

---

5. REAL STUDENTS IN ACTION

What's Here for You

Many of us want to see how something is done. If you are one of these people, this is your chapter. We just finished <u>talking</u> about how to write a high scoring essay. Now we will <u>show</u> how five essays were written using **The No-Study Solution**© in the "heat of battle" and <u>observe</u> the <u>grade</u> <u>achieved</u>.

Mostly, I left the essays as the student wrote them originally. This gives you a sense of what a <u>realistic</u> <u>effort</u> looks like, an effort under real-world constraints of time and range of skills across grade levels. Since <u>actual</u> <u>students</u> wrote these essays, <u>not professional</u> <u>educators</u>, it is realistic to assume that you too can achieve similar results and similar grades.

Our graded essays feature students from 15 years to 28 years old, enrolled in classes from High School to Graduate School. They span subjects from English through Science to Economics. We begin presenting each essay with a profile of the student, the question they answered and the techniques they used. Then we present the essay. Alongside the essay itself, we show how the student applied each **PERFORMANCE SECRET**, **STRATEGY TOOL** or **MODEL**. We point out exactly where and how the student used the techniques. I believe this section is probably the first time such a clear and revealing step-by-step illustration of how to write high scoring essays has ever been released to the general public. For this reason, I also believe that Chapter 5 is the most valuable section of the book for anyone serious about improving their grades.

While essays II, III and V are the personal efforts of the author, essays I and IV are the work of my niece and nephew respectively. Meanwhile, the "Cat is Better" Essay, **Cats Rule, Dogs Drool**, is the personal effort of my sister. This gives the reader exposure to four different writing styles. I am grateful for their courage to display both their genius and flaws for your benefit – the reader. Our line-up of essays and the key technique each essay demonstrates is:

  I. **What Ancient Rome Could Teach Romeo and Juliet** (T-View Outline©)
  II. **Task Force** (The Design – First Writing Model)
  III. **Risk** (The Point Stack© – Second Writing Model)
  IV. **The Future of Science** (The Nail Down© – Third Writing Model)
  V. **New Airport in Chicago** (Engaging the Reader)

I. **What Ancient Rome Could Teach Romeo and Juliet**
(T-View Outline©)

Subject:	English Literature
Level:	High School, Junior Year
School:	North Star Scholar Academy
Age:	15
Gender:	Female
Hometown:	Syracuse, UT
Scores:	3.95 GPA
Test Question:	*Could the tragedy of Romeo and Juliet have been avoided? If so, how?*
Test:	Essay, open book
Grade on Essay:	A
Example of:	– STRATEGY TOOL #2: Use the T-View Outline© to capture the best ideas, outline the essay and see both sides of an issue, pages 36-40. – The Idea Stack©, page 91. – Writing from an Idea Stack©, page 118. – The Single-Thought-Thesis© technique, pages 81-82.

Student's **T-View Outline**© reproduced here in its entirety:

AVOID	CAN'T AVOID
1- HONESTY BEST	NATURAL CHARACTER FLAWS
12- LINCOLN, WASHINGTON, SHAKESPEARE	FATE IN TIMING
4- TELL PARENTS	FATE / CIRCUMSTANCES
2- ROMEO NOT KILL	POTION WORE OFF TOO LATE
5- JULIET AVOID Ro	FEUD TOO STRONG
3- DON'T FAKE DIE	
6- FEUD STUPID/SPEAK OUT	SHAKESPEARE SELLS MORE TICKETS WITH TRAGEDY
10- NURSE TELL PARENTS	PRIEST NOT HONEST
11- NURSE NOT HELP	NURSE HID TRUTH
8- DON'T MARRY THEM	ROMEO TOO IMPULSIVE
9- LEADERSHIP	PEOPLE RUN BY EMOTIONS
7- DON'T MIX POTION	

Student chose to argue the left side of the "T"; that the tragedy was avoidable, having viewed both sides of the argument and weighed the strength of each position.

What Ancient Rome Could Teach Romeo and Juliet

A keystone is the rock that fits in the top of an arch and holds it together. It was invented by the Romans to hold their aqueducts together, without it the arches would have crashed to the ground. Honesty is a keystone character trait that holds people's lives together. Dishonesty is the reason for two young lovers lying dead in a tomb at the end of the play. If Romeo and Juliet had been honest, they would have lived.

> Describe thesis in a single thought, p. 81.

Honesty[1] is the best policy. Look at all the problems that arose because two kids didn't tell the truth. Killing[2] someone because your great-grandfathers killed each other isn't honest. Romeo got married against his parent's wishes, which is not honest. Romeo could have bridled his passion and told Juliet that he was determined to keep his reputation and not marry her yet or not at all. That would have showed remarkable honesty of heart and mind.

1 – Honesty Best

2 – Romeo not kill

Juliet pretended[3] to be dead instead of just telling her parents that she was already married. She was not honest. If Romeo and Juliet had told[4] Mom and Dad that they were married Mr. and Mrs. Capulet would not have tried to make Juliet marry Paris. If Juliet had told her parents there might have been some hard feelings for a while but in the end, the marriage could have brought the two families together.

3 – Don't Fake Die

4 – Tell Parents

After Juliet found out he was a Montague she could have decided that she didn't want to be involved[5] in a relationship with him out of honesty to her family. Furthermore, she could have been forthright[6] with her family about her feelings for Romeo, helping them to see the futility in their feud. This would have showed great honesty on her part.

5 - Juliet Avoid Romeo

6 - Feud Stupid, Speak Out

Throughout the story, there are people that could have helped Romeo and Juliet be honest. One such character is the old priest that married them secretly and made the potion⁷ so Juliet could pretend to be dead *"Presently through all thy veins shall run a cold and drowsy humor, for no pulse shall...testify thou livest."* Friar Laurence being an adult and a priest was accountable. He could have refused⁸ to marry them without the parent's permission or knowledge. He could have tried to talk Romeo out of his passion. He could have encouraged⁹ the couple to tell their parents about the marriage. When Juliet came begging at his door after Romeo was banished for killing Tybalt he could have told her she got herself into that mess she could get herself out. He never had to make the potion.

"There's no trust, no faith, no honesty in men; all perjured all forsworn, all naught, all dissemblers" says Juliet's nurse who was just as dishonest. She knew all about Romeo and the marriage, but instead of telling¹⁰ the Capulet family like an honest nurse would have, she helped¹¹ Romeo and Juliet in their dishonesty the whole time. If the friar and the nurse had been honest and counseled the young couple in truth they would have chosen a better course of action and gone on to live full long lives.

The nurse and the friar had the opportunity to lead the young people to better decisions prior to the culminating dual suicide. *"I will be brief for my short date of breath is not so long as this tedious tale."* The friar says in the end when he is caught at the tomb where Romeo and Juliet are both dead. He was then sentenced to death because he dishonestly helped the teens. Right there it tells you that he could have been honest because it was expected.

Contrast Romeo, Juliet, the nurse and friar to George Washington, Abraham Lincoln (hence the name honest Abe) and Shakespeare¹². Believe it or not even Shakespeare said, *"No legacy is so rich as honesty."* (All's well that ends well). The reason these three people were great was because they were honest, and they were trusted with leadership. They lived a long time.

7 – Don't Make Potion

8 – Don't Marry Them

9 – Leadership

10 – Nurse Tell Parents

11 – Nurse Not Help

12 – Lincoln, Washington, Shakespeare

You may ask if Shakespeare believed his words, *"no legacy is so rich as honesty"* seeing that he wrote a play about dishonesty. Shakespeare wrote it to prove the point that honesty is better than dishonesty. Smart people learn from their mistakes, wise people learn from <u>all</u> their mistakes. <u>If Romeo and Juliet had made better choices and been honest with the people around them, and if the adults they confided in had been honest, they would have lived.</u> As we apply the lessons taught by Shakespeare in this play, we won't be dishonest like they were. *"Some will be pardoned some punished: for never was a story of more woe than this of Juliet and her Romeo."*

Notice how the conclusion mirrors the thesis statement, p. 145.

II. Task Force (The Design – First Writing Model)

Subject: English Composition
Level: College, Junior Year, Honors Program
School: Brigham Young University

Age: 21
Gender: Male
Hometown: Paxton, MA
Scores: ACT 28

Assignment: Write an essay on a subject of classification.
Value: 12.5% of course grade
Grade on Essay: A -

Example of: – PERFORMANCE SECRET #15: Explain the thesis three times: Tell them what you are going to tell them, Tell them, Tell them what you told them, page 109.
– When to Write What Guide©, page 133.

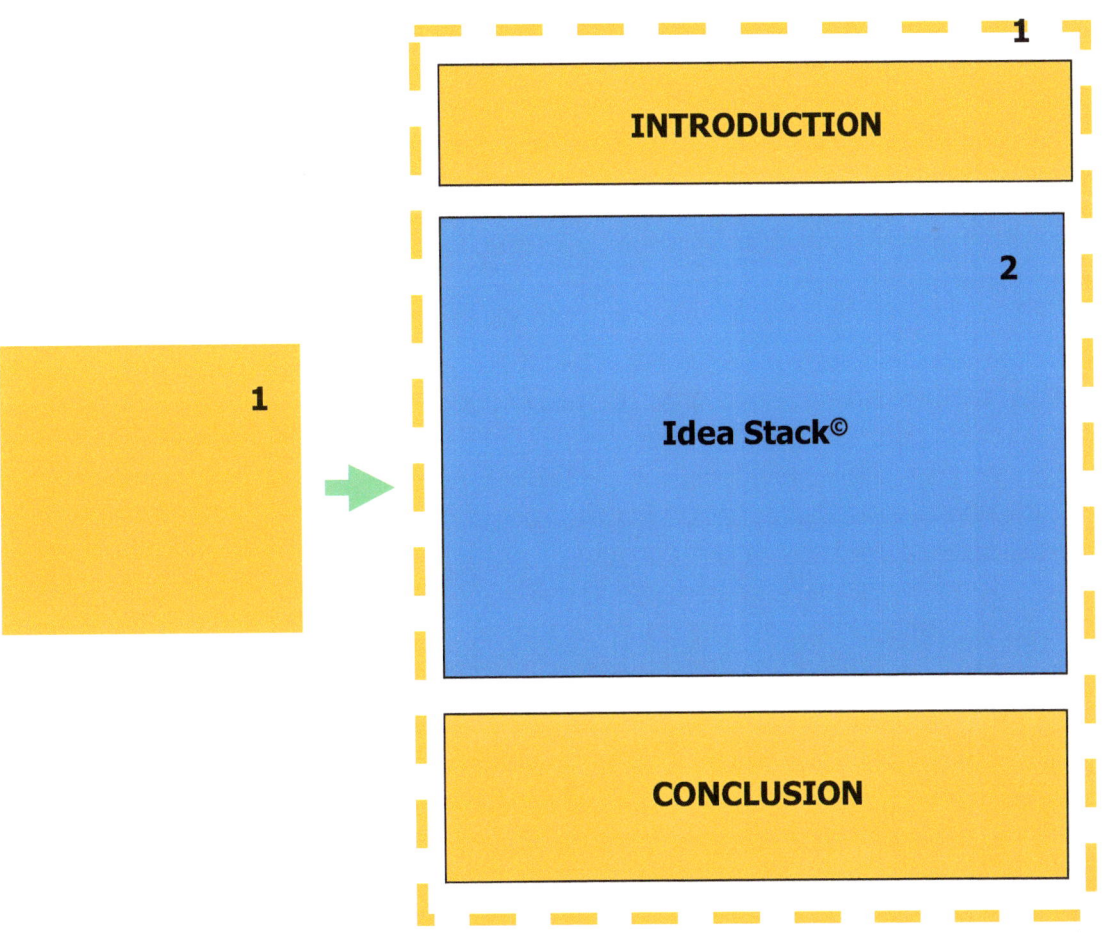

Task Force

During the Second World War, the United States created the largest navy in the history of the world. It succeeded in combat not only because of its sheer numbers, but also through organization into task forces, which are a balanced group of the four basic types of surface warships. Although the ships were all composed of the same materials, their physical design characteristics created different individual capabilities that enabled each to contribute a necessary part of the whole.

> **INTRODUCTION**
>
> **Thesis Statement**

At the center of the task force sailed the **aircraft carrier**. Rather awkward in appearance aircraft carriers resembled a floating shoe box with a little house on top. Usually displacing 27,100 tons, an Essex class carrier housed a strike force of 103 planes. The weight of airplane hangars, repair shops, magazines, weapons, fuel and crew left little provision for armor. A walkway hung over the sea below the edge of the flight deck. Engineers jammed this trench full of 20 mm and 40 mm quadruple anti-aircraft guns. Even so, the carrier relied primarily on its speed and defending fighter aircraft to protect itself by evading torpedoes and shooting down enemy bombers. The carrier contributed to the task force by delivering its air-striking power.

Before the war, navy experts expected the **battleship** to determine the outcome of fleet actions. The sinking of the HMS Prince of Wales and HMS Repulse ended that idea. However, the battleships turned out to be the best ship design for the role of anti-aircraft defense for the aircraft carriers. Thick armor belts and heavily plated decks made the battleships impregnable against the usual Japanese 500-lb or 1,000-lb aerial bomb, and especially against the Kamikazes. A South Dakota or North Carolina class battleship displaced 35,000 tons and housed nine sixteen inch guns, sixteen to twenty 5" guns in dual mounts and 15-19 40 mm quadruple mount anti-aircraft guns. As menacing as a porcupine, this concentration of firepower allowed few hostile planes

> **2**
>
> **Idea Stack©**
>
> There are four ideas in this Idea Stack©
>
> 1. Aircraft Carriers
> 2. Battleships
> 3. Cruisers
> 4. Destroyers

to pass through. Battleships sailed closest to the carriers, providing the first ring of defense for the valuable aircraft carrier. By operating close by, the battleship's firepower and armor compensated for the weaknesses inherent in the aircraft carrier. The battleship contributed to the taskforce by delivering close range defensive and offensive firepower.

    Sheer size brought two detrimental effects on both the battleship and aircraft carrier – cost and time to build. Much smaller, **cruisers** could be built more quickly and still provide anti-aircraft protection. A Baltimore class heavy cruiser displaced 13,600 tons, possessed sleeker lines, and was faster than most battleships. On the decks sat twelve 5-inch guns, numerous 40 mm quads, and the nine-gun 8" main battery. In a pinch, cruisers could deliver close range firepower. More abundant than their larger contemporaries, cruisers sailed adjacent to the battleships in ring formation. The cruisers contributed the second ring of defense to the taskforce by delivering anti-aircraft defense seemingly everywhere – all the time.

    Too large to outmaneuver submarines, the previously mentioned ships could not defend themselves against their submersible enemies. The Fletcher class **destroyer** displaced 2,050 tons and rode close to the water, bringing its ten torpedoes and anti-submarine weapons down to the water level. Destroyers sailed the furthest out from the carriers in the third ring of defense in order to perform their anti-submarine duties. Sensitive sonar sets on the bridge, "Hedge Hog" mounts amidships, and depth charges on the fantail combined to locate and destroy enemy subs. Their lack of any armor earned destroyers the nickname "Tin Can." Lightness and powerful engines made destroyers the fastest warships in the task force. Many could make 35 knots, two knots better than the fastest aircraft carriers. The destroyer's small size allowed for maneuverability over a submerged enemy sub. If such a thing as gas mileage existed for ships, the EPA would rate destroyers best. Each destroyer housed

Idea Stack©
continued

five 5-inch guns and a dozen 40 mm quads. "Tin Cans" contributed to the task force by defending against under sea attack and low flying enemy aircraft.

As shown above, these four types of ships, **aircraft carrier**, **battleship**, **cruiser** and **destroyer** were uniquely different in size and capabilities. Just as an orchestra needs all of its instruments to perform a symphony successfully, the task force needed each type of ship playing its part. It was the design of these different ships working together as a task force that helped each survive individually and made the United States Navy taskforce collectively unbeatable on the open sea.

> **Brief Detail** - A short review of key findings that prove the thesis, page 133.

> **CONCLUSION**

> Notice there are no new insights here, just deepening of original thesis. See WARNING, p. 145.

III.   Risk (The Idea Stack© - Second Writing Model)

Subject:	English Composition
Level:	College, Junior Year, Honors Program
School:	Brigham Young University

Age:	21
Gender:	Male
Hometown:	Paxton, MA
Scores:	ACT 28

Assignment:	Write an essay using three stories to prove your thesis.
Value:	12.5% of course grade
Grade on Essay:	A

Example of: – WRITING MODEL #2: The Idea Stack© lists all the ideas and numbers them in the most convincing order.
– PERFORMANCE SECRET #16: Present three ideas in support of a thesis in order to satisfy the grader's sub-conscious checklist. (Note: stories used as ideas)
– PERFORMANCE SECRET #22: Use a story to deliver an idea with powerful emotional impact.
– PERFORMANCE SECRET #19: Grab the reader's attention …by cutting to the action…

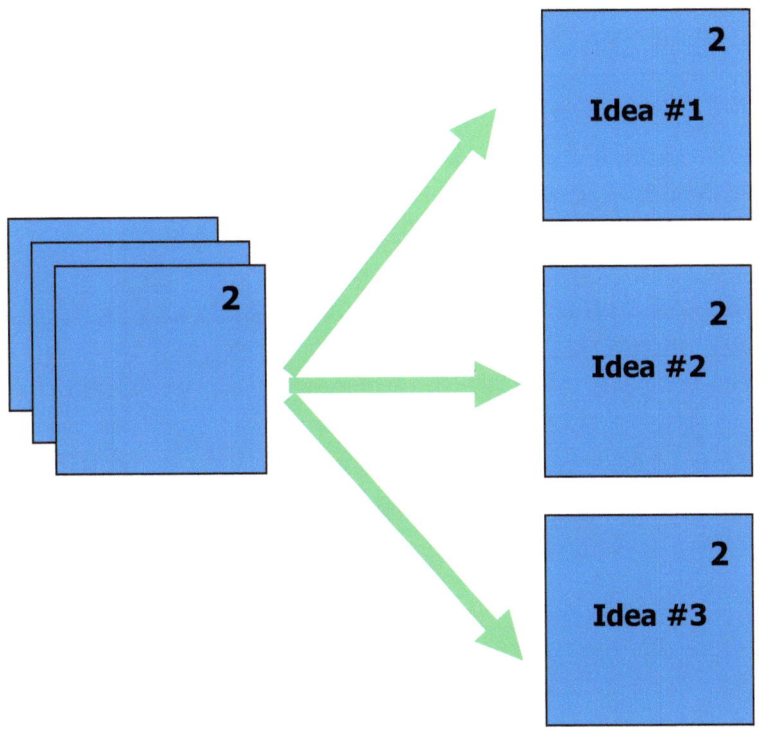

Risk

<u>Inside Las Vegas casinos, a human drama is unfolding as people win fortunes and lose paychecks</u>. This drama is a microcosm of how people determine their destinies. It seems paradoxical that an environment fabricated by luck and chance could personify man's use of freedom of choice.

> **Student grabs attention with a cut to the action, p. 136.**

These players use so many different strategies; you wonder which one is the best. Conservative players stop immediately after registering a small gain. They hold on to this money with as much tenacity as old ladies who clutch their pocketbooks when they are being mugged. Across the table, sit the more adventurous gamblers. Remembering great fortunes won in the past, they take risks that produce huge sums of money. Invariably they roll the dice one too many times, and lose all their money. When the game is finished, many players wonder what they could have had, had they taken the chances offered them. A great question lingers in their minds, "Should I have taken bigger risks?"

No one ever got the best of a business deal when he dealt with Grandpa Donnelly. Grandpa, a successful real estate entrepreneur and purchasing agent for the Baltimore & Ohio Railroad, made his million before the Great Depression. The Donnellys lived a very comfortable life during that gloomy decade. On a warm June evening in 1932, the Donnelly home was extravagantly prepared for their son's wedding the following day. Out on the front porch Grandpa talked privately to his son. "How do you really feel about tomorrow, Scott?" "Well, father, to be honest with you, I don't really love her. However, I know what calling off the engagement now would do to your reputation. Besides, who knows if I could ever find a better woman than Sally, she's a remarkable person, so I'll go through with it."

> **2**
> **Idea #1**
>
> **Scott did not take a risk in life and the result was loss of true love.**

180

The No-Study Solution! – Writing Essays

Lieutenant Commander Clarence W. McClusky flew high above the Pacific Ocean on the morning of June 4, 1942. The leader of two dive-bomber squadrons, he was rather perplexed because the Japanese fleet was not where Intelligence said it would be. McClusky had to make a decision. His bombers were low on fuel and would soon have to return to the U.S.S. Enterprise or crash land into the sea. McClusky knew he must find the Japanese carriers in rearming condition before they could strike, but where could they be? Other squadrons flying alongside McClusky chose to fly straight on south to land on Midway Island. Risking his planes and his pilots, McClusky chose to go neither to Midway nor to the Enterprise. He flew north on a hunch that the enemy had sailed in that direction to refuel. Minutes later he was rewarded by the sight of smoke on the horizon. Gradually ships began to appear under each column of smoke. When he was completely over the fleet, he could hardly believe his eyes. Without any delay, McClusky pushed the nose of his plane over to dive-bomb the Japanese aircraft carriers. Leading 37 planes, McClusky was able to destroy two carriers and win the battle. Although some of his planes ran out of gas on the way home, their crews were rescued later. The risk had paid off.

Idea #2

McClusky risked all of his planes and men. He won the battle and changed the balance of power in the world.

On his way to the University cafeteria, Mark, a sophomore, paused to read a paper stapled to a bulletin board. It was entitled, "Ten Keys to Success." Step Six read: ***"Take risks. What is the worst thing that can happen to you if you take the risk? If you can live with that, take the risk."*** Mark went over to his mailbox and pulled out a letter written by his girlfriend back home. They had known each other a long time. Mark didn't know how much he loved her because he was too shy to get to know anybody else. As Mark walked over into line, he began opening the letter. The girl standing in front of him seemed really attractive and friendly. Mark just stood there for a minute. Then he put the letter back in his pocket and said, *"This snow we're having sure is neat, don't you think?"*

Mark takes a risk that may lead to a new romantic relationship.

Idea #3

The Teacher's instructions are met with 3 stories. The writer leaves the outcome up to the reader's imagination for dramatic effect.

IV. **The Future of Science** (The Nail Down© – Third Writing Model)

Subject: Research Methods & Laboratory Science
Level: Graduate School, First Year
School: University of Illinois at Urbana-Champaign

Age: 19
Gender: Male
Hometown: Columbus, OH
Scores: GRE 800 Math / 640 Verbal

Assignment: Write an essay on the significance of research
Grade on Essay: Pass

Example of:
– WRITING MODEL #3: The Nail Down© writes each idea by **D**escribing it, **P**roving it and telling why it is **I**mportant.
– STRATEGY TOOL #7: Use all Three Layers simultaneously
– PERFORMANCE SECRET #17: Tell the reader why each idea is important. Do not leave it up to the reader to figure out.

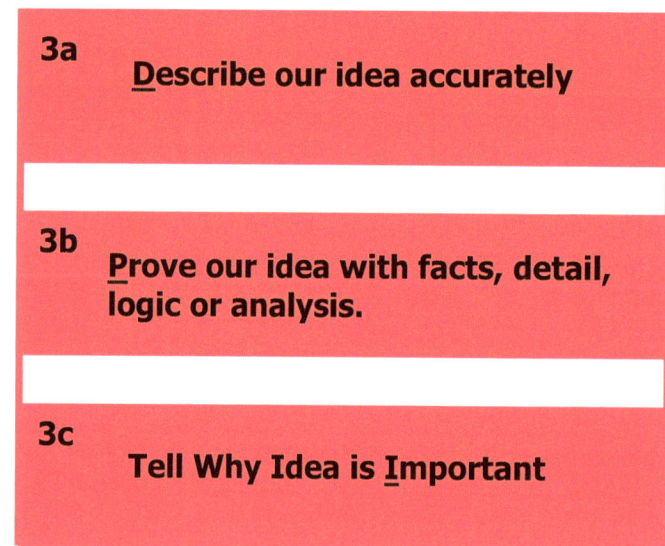

The Future of Science: The Quantitative Revolution

Throughout the ages, man has been satisfied by qualitative descriptions; Fungus grows in moist environments. It gets hot during the day and cold at night. These are valuable, important, and have served us well. However, as time has gone on, needs have changed. No longer is a description accurate: there simply isn't enough information. We not only need to know what it is, but how much! ← **Thesis Statement**

Since Galileo's study of the constant acceleration and quadratic position function of masses and Newton's Principia Mathematica, we have learned the universe obeys fundamental rules. As logical and illogical as they may seem, those, which stand the rigorous tests of experiment and statistical methods, are accepted conditionally as truths. This "quantitative revolution" has been or is taking place in every field of science. ← **Idea #1** (2)

There are fields such as physics, engineering, and mathematics, which are fundamentally quantitative. Chemistry as a more recent field, having received a charge from Immanuel Kant in the 1700s, is now deeply rooted in analysis. Geography was after that. Most recently, however, changes in biological sciences, from physiology, to genetics have uprooted our preconceptions on the nature of life and the universe. This empirical change has allowed us to make discoveries of qualitative nature that could never have been done, such as validating Einstein's relativity or creating a working engine.

3a Describe idea #1
Identifies quantitative disciplines

3b Prove idea #1
Uses three facts: Chemistry, Geography, and Biology

3c Why Important
Discoveries such as Einstein's now possible

In chemistry, a similar revolution took place. While quantitative measurements were always taken, such as the weight of a set of compounds, exactness in the science was not always. Beginning in the 1700s with chemists Lavoisier, chemistry took to itself anew a rigor which would serve it well for the centuries to come. With the conservation of mass, instead of simply reporting the qualitative results of an experiment, ideas such as entropy, energy, heat, and temperature could be defined, studied, and understood. More importantly, however, a standardized system of units permitted a scientific community with peer review and generalized language to work together. Such principles have been crucial in the development of science since.

While Biology has been described as the study of the extremely complex, this aptly describes the immensity of the pool of knowledge. Most illustrative of the "quantitative revolution" is a comparison of modern and pre-modern experiments in Biology. In biology, this revolution was spawned by the availability of new technology.

Leeuwenhoek, in the 1600s, discovered cells through the manipulation of an optical microscope.

He used the best instruments available in his time, and he learned a great deal about the nature of life. However, the information he collected was limited.

Carlos Bustamente, using Ashkin's invention of the optical tweezers, was able to quantify the size of steps on specific DNA-binding proteins. This involved enormous amounts of information, and instead of learning more with less information, it's a matter of finding specific answers from a complete overload of information.

These breakthroughs have now become a system by which scientists learn about the world in which we exist. A system that is more detailed, descriptive and packed with important information. Scientists test and retest theirs and others experiments for verification and extrapolation. Due to the peer-reviewed system, we are able to eliminate errors and find clear answers to questions. Errors, in principle, should be discovered by either peer review or subsequent verification. <u>Due to the change towards a quantitative system, our understanding of the world and control thereof has been irreversibly changed and this may be as important as the industrial revolution.</u>

Conclusion

V. New Airport in Chicago (Engaging the Reader)

Subject: Micro Economics
Level: Graduate School
School: University of Chicago

Age: 28
Gender: Male
Hometown: Paxton, MA
Scores: GMAT 610

Test: Final Exam, in class, timed, 45 minutes allocated
Test Question: *Given three options, where should the Mayor of Chicago build a new airport?*
Grade on Essay: A

Example of:
– STRATEGY TOOL #9: Use the HIT© approach to write an engaging and convincing Introduction.
– PERFORMANCE SECRET #6: Find deep insights by identifying the Potential Changes in the System.
– STRATEGY TOOL #4: Defuse with The Direct Approach© by using a *Because, State Evidence* or *Comparison*.
– PERFORMANCE SECRET #17: Tell the reader why each idea is important. Do not leave it up to the reader to figure out.
– PERFORMANCE SECRET #21: Use a table to show that you have accounted for all the key information, to communicate the deep meaning of ideas and to cover more in less time.
– PERFORMANCE SECRET #2: The first action to take when writing an essay is not to write anything at all. The first action is to THINK.

New Airport in Chicago

[Mayor Daley is faced with a tough decision given three choices.][1] [There is competition among the airports for traffic and freight] [2], [so the airport must be put in a location where Demand can support an airport operating at the lowest point on its survival curve.][3]

> **HIT©**
> [1] **H**ello Sentence
> [2] **I**ssue/Key Principle
> [3] **T**hesis
> Page 135

Costs have two components: Fixed and Variable. Fixed costs are primarily Capital to construct the airport. Truly, the Kankakee farmland will be the lowest cost because real estate is cheap relative to the south side of Chicago – because the opportunity cost is to do nothing with the land except wait 50 years for urban sprawl to reach it. South East Chicago will be expensive to buy from all the economic agents using the land today, however, <u>if an island can be created cheaply in Lake Michigan, say a floating island like an aircraft carrier, it may have lower construction costs</u> than South East Chicago.

> **Identifying the Potential Change in the System, p. 57.**
>
> The student introduces a system change of his own by eliminating the need for land on shore to handle the runways and taxiways for aircraft.

Variable costs should be the same for all airports in fuel and electricity but labor costs will differ because for people to be hired competitively, they can't spend a lot of money to get to work. Making this assumption people will live close to work. It will be hard to find Labor in Kankakee because the small supply will bid up the price. South East Chicago will have rather flat supply costs as will Downtown Chicago.

<u>The cost of building the airport is a fixed cost and eventually will become a minute piece of the ATC [Average Total Cost], so it may pay in the long run to build the island.</u> The goal of having competitive costs is to land at the minimum on the LRATC [Long Range Average Total Cost] Curve, to get there, output must be healthy.

> **Defuse with The Direct Approach© by using a *State Evidence*, p. 65.**
>
> Negate the superior low cost of non-Chicago Loop land options with the truth about fixed cost over time (that it becomes zero).

Kankakee will have fewer people desiring flights there because it is over an hour drive from Chicago. South East is located in a large population but may suffer from competition from Midway

International Airport and an artificial island located off the loop could tap the downtown population with little substitution effect from O'Hare International Airport.

The Key effect of putting the airport in Chicago is the increased demand for complementary goods and services to the airport and increased employment in the vicinity of the airport. An airport also nets taxes from operations and real estate taxes to Mayor Daley's budget. Where the airport is built does not affect which contractor gets the job, hence, the construction cost should not be considered an economic advantage to Chicago contractors.

In conclusion, I would like to rank the three alternatives in the following table: (Ranking is ordinate where supported by the essay; otherwise YES / NO where feature is binary).

> **Tell the reader why each idea is important. Do not leave it up to the reader to figure out, p. 129.**

Why this location is more important than either of the other locations

> **Use a table to show that you have accounted for the key information, to convey the deep meaning of ideas, page 142.**

	South East Chicago	Floating Island Loop	Kankakee Farmland
Fixed Cost	3	2	1
Variable Cost	Same	Same	Same
Labor (Subset of Variable Cost)	2	3	1
Demand for Flights	2	1	3
Substitution by nearby Airport (yes is bad)	YES	NO	NO
Boost to complementary businesses in Chicago	YES	YES	NO
Boost to employment (Chicago residents)	YES	YES	NO
Chicago Tax Revenue	YES	YES	NO

In summary, you need demand for flights to get to low LRATC [Long Range Average Total Cost] and Mayor Daley wants the Airport in Chicago for the economic advantages of revenue, therefore build the artificial island off the Chicago Loop.

> **The first action you take when writing an essay is not to write anything at all. The first action is to THINK.**

Writing an essay with an accurate and complete table of ideas (costs and economic factors) is only possible after THINK and STAGE completed. This essay's "live" test notes appear on the next page.

Actual THINK and STAGE Notes I scratched on the last page of the exam booklet, before writing this essay, notice how I wrote down "**My** <u>**Notes**</u>" in case my professor wondered if they were part of the essay or not:

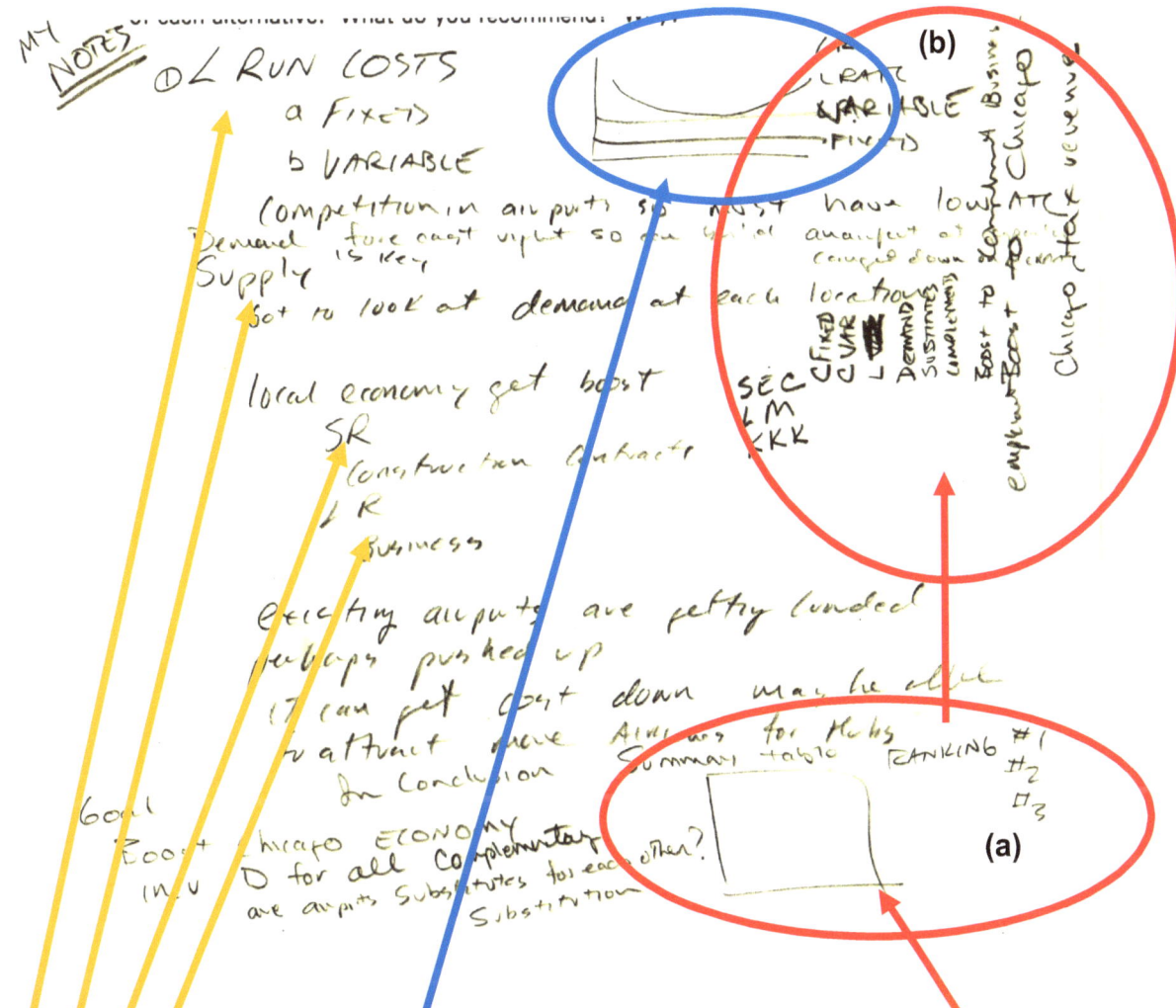

Student thought up the key ideas, listed them in an Idea Stack©

Picture provides student with visual of Key Issue/Principle he is describing, the Long Range Average Total Cost. See Performance Secret #20 – Use a Diagram as a memory device, p. 141-142.

The table starts as an idea to rank all three locations (a), it is later fleshed out as the student figures out the headers for the row and columns in (b), final version on p. 188.

6. FUNCTIONAL INDEX

System Views:

> **THE ONE SYSTEM: The No-Study Solution© for Writing Essays**
> Page 24

> **The No-Study Solution© for Writing Essays - Concept View**
> Page 154

> **The No-Study Solution© for Writing Essays - Strategy View**
> Page 155

> **Strategy Map for Writing Our Essay**
> Page 102

The No-Study Solution! – Writing Essays

Strategy Tools:

STRATEGY TOOL #1: Walk into the exam with a game plan:
   1st – Think
   2nd – Stage
   3rd – Write

Page 21

STRATEGY TOOL #2: Use the T-View Outline© to capture the best ideas, outline the essay and see both sides of an issue.

Page 36

STRATEGY TOOL #3: Create a rationally sound essay by looking for gaps in four areas:
   - **B**reakdowns in logic
   - **U**niversal principles in play
   - **G**laring weaknesses
   - **S**ystem changes

Page 44

STRATEGY TOOL #4: Defuse with The Direct Approach© by using a *Because, State Evidence* or *Comparison*.

Page 64

STRATEGY TOOL #5: Defuse with The Replacement Approach© by presenting a better idea in place of the opposing strength.

Page 68

STRATEGY TOOL #6: Use the Timing Ladder© to know when to start writing, when to switch from one idea to the next, and when to stop writing.

Page 92

STRATEGY TOOL #7: Use all Three Layers simultaneously to achieve a persuasive argument that proves your thesis.

Page 132

STRATEGY TOOL #8: Use the When to Write What Guide© to select the type of information to place within each section of the essay.

Page 133

STRATEGY TOOL #9: Use the HIT© approach to write an engaging and credible Introduction.
- **H**ello Sentence
- **I**ssue / Key Principle Sentence
- **T**hesis Sentence

Page 135

Performance Secrets:

PERFORMANCE SECRET #0: Use the 3 keys to crossing a street safely, to remember the 3 keys to write an essay effectively.
Page 5

PERFORMANCE SECRET #1: View taking tests as playing a game. Love playing that game.
Page 14

PERFORMANCE SECRET #2: The first action to take when writing an essay is not to write anything at all. The first action is to THINK.
Page 32

PERFORMANCE SECRET #3: Achieve common sense by being <u>c</u>urious and asking *"How does this work?"*
Page 45

PERFORMANCE SECRET #4: Avoid trick questions by identifying the <u>U</u>niversal principles and the boundaries they operate within.
Page 49

PERFORMANCE SECRET #5: Identify <u>G</u>laring weaknesses by asking: *"Who does this idea benefit the most? Us or Them?"*
Page 54

PERFORMANCE SECRET #6: Find deep insights by identifying the potential changes *already there* in the <u>S</u>ystem.
Page 57

PERFORMANCE SECRET #7: Use the First THINK /Second THINK approach to find the defuse to a dangerous counter-idea.
Page 62

PERFORMANCE SECRET #8: Choose the "other" side when it delivers a more persuasive argument.

Page 72

PERFORMANCE SECRET #9: Allow the ideas to show the way to your thesis. Find the invincible idea and use it as the foundation for your thesis.

Page 80

PERFORMANCE SECRET #10: Use the Single-Thought-Thesis© technique to simplify your thesis down to one thought.

Page 81

PERFORMANCE SECRET #11: Use the Hierarchy of Strength to achieve maximum persuasive impact. Present ideas in declining order, strongest first to weakest last.

Page 86

PERFORMANCE SECRET #12: Use the Building Upon Prior Ideas sequence when one idea requires an idea established before it, or when proof depends upon chronological order of ideas.

Page 88

PERFORMANCE SECRET #13: If an idea does not advance the strength of your thesis – toss it out!

Page 90

PERFORMANCE SECRET #14: Split time into two blocks:
   1 - THINK/STAGE
   2 - WRITE

Page 94

> **PERFORMANCE SECRET #15:** Explain the thesis three times:
> 1st - Tell them what you are going to tell them
> 2nd - Tell them
> 3rd - Tell them what you told them
>
> **Page 109**

> **PERFORMANCE SECRET #16:** Present three ideas in support of your thesis in order to satisfy the grader's subconscious checklist.
>
> **Page 119**

> **PERFORMANCE SECRET #17:** Tell the reader why each idea is important. Do not leave it up to the reader to figure out.
>
> **Page 129**

> **PERFORMANCE SECRET #18:** Relate to the reader on an emotional level. Consider what he will <u>see</u>, <u>hear</u> and <u>feel</u>. Write in a manner and mood that appeals to the reader.
>
> **Page 134**

> **PERFORMANCE SECRET #19:** Grab the reader's attention by connecting to the human experience, cutting to the action and using Clever-Thought-Twists©.
>
> **Page 135**

> **PERFORMANCE SECRET #20:** Draw a diagram to recall a complete set of information and to provide an illustration for your essay.
>
> **Page 140**

> **PERFORMANCE SECRET #21:** Use a table to show that you have accounted for the key information, to communicate the deep meaning of ideas and to cover more in less time.
>
> **Page 142**

> **PERFORMANCE SECRET #22:** Use a story to deliver an idea with powerful emotional impact.
>
> **Page 143**

> **PERFORMANCE SECRET #23:** Clean up your handwriting by double spacing, slowing down, changing the angle or printing.
>
> **Page 146**

> **PERFORMANCE SECRET #24:** Find the Point of Leverage by asking the question, *"What makes this work?"*
>
> **Page 162**

> **PERFORMANCE SECRET #25:** Know what you want.
>
> **Page 165**

Writing Models:

> **WRITING MODEL #1:** The Design consists of an Introduction, an Idea Stack© and a Conclusion.
>
> **Page 109**

> **WRITING MODEL #2:** The Idea Stack© lists all the ideas and numbers them in the most convincing order.
>
> **Page 117**

> **WRITING MODEL #3:** The Nail Down© writes each idea by **D**escribing it, **P**roving it and telling why it is **I**mportant.
>
> **Page 123**

Mark Hopkins has twenty years' experience in Human Learning and Performance with a specialty in computer-delivered learning and skill assessment systems.

He designed and implemented multimedia learning classrooms throughout high schools in the State of Utah, the Colorado Community College system, and at a number of campuses within the University of Texas and Texas A&M systems. The Utah project garnered his team the 1998 Governor's Award from the Utah State House of Representatives. In the Department of Defense, Mark consulted with the U.S. Army and U.S. Air Force Training Commands on the development of software driven instructional design engines and training delivery platforms. In the private sector, Mark worked with executives at Charles Schwab, Freightliner Trucks, Oracle, Warner Bros., Fleet Bank, ExxonMobil, Bell Helicopter Textron, Lockheed Martin, Texas Instruments and United, American and Continental Airlines on the development of learning and skill assessment strategies for improving the training, performance and evaluation of their employees.

While working on many of these projects, Mark saw a huge disparity between the learning tools available to teachers, parents and students in the educational arena and those he was delivering to corporations in America. He desperately wanted the everyday student to have access to powerful tools that could change their skill levels and propel them into fulfilling careers. So he wrote **The No-Study Solution**© which delivers an industrial quality solution to the educational space. Unlike most works in the educational self-help study genre, the examples of "A" essays in **The No-Study Solution**© are not written by professional educators, but rather by students in school who scored A's on those papers in the American education system.

For the first time, the art of writing a high-scoring essay is broken down sentence-by-sentence and paragraph-by-paragraph showing the student or parent how to write clearly and effectively while telling the teacher what they want to hear to receive their "A" grade. A successful student himself, Mark tested out of his Freshman year by the end of his first week in college, went on to earn his BS at Brigham Young University in three years and later studied MBA courses at the University of Chicago. His Major GPA at BYU was 3.74. His GPA while enrolled in the University of Chicago MBA/190 program was 4.0. Professionally, he completed the yearlong IBM Marketing Training Program in the top 98% of his sales class and graduated an IBM Systems Engineer.

www.ingramcontent.com/pod-product-compliance
Lightning Source LLC
Chambersburg PA
CBHW040910020526
44116CB00026B/17